Barron's Head Start to College

DATE DUE	
June 1, 2009	

About the Author

Susan Chiarolanzio is the Director of College Counseling at Flint Hill School in Oakton, Virginia. She spent ten years working in the admissions departments of Gettysburg College (PA), Drew University (NJ), and Georgetown University (Washington, D.C.). This is her first book for Barron's.

© Copyright 2004 by Barron's Educational Series, Inc.

All inquiries should be addressed to:
Barron's Educational Series, Inc.
250 Wireless Boulevard
Hauppauge, New York 11788
http://www.barronseduc.com

Library of Congress Catalog Card No. 2004041102

International Standard Book No. 0-7641-2697-0

Library of Congress Cataloging-in-Publication Data
Chiarolanzio, Susan.
    Barron's Head Start to College Planning / Susan Chiarolanzio.
        p. cm.
    ISBN 0-7641-2697-0 (alk. paper)
    1. Universities and colleges—Admission. 2. College choice. I. Title

LB2351.C43 2004
378.1'61'0973—dc22
                                                      2004041102

Printed in the United States of America
9 8 7 6 5 4 3 2 1

Contents

Introduction

Each year, in my role as a college counselor in a rigorous, independent school, I receive several phone calls from the parents of younger children or from those considering enrolling their children at the school, wondering about the college acceptances for the current seniors. Some of the motivation for these calls is genuine curiosity about how our senior class has fared in the college search process. At some level, though, their motivation is wondering if they've made the right decision about sending their child to an independent school, a need for reassurance that when the time comes, their child will get into a "good" college, and a desire to learn what they can do now to help their child find that right school. In the fast-paced achievement-oriented world we live in, sometimes parents forget that their kids are just kids and each stage of childhood is worthwhile and meaningful in its own right, not just a stop on their way to the next one. They want to push quickly through some of the preliminary steps of growing up to get to what they view as the ultimate stage—college. Of course, whatever parents do, they do out of concern and love for their children. This book is designed to help these caring and concerned parents make sense out of a process that is rapidly and constantly changing and is both complex and unknown.

Playing the role of the outsider is uncomfortable. Unfortunately, most parents looking ahead to the college search process for their children feel completely unprepared and often out of the loop. Instinctively, parents who feel out of control over some aspect of their children's lives, especially one perceived to be crucial to their children's futures, will take action, doing anything in their power to regain a sense of security. A little information can go a long way in reassuring parents that the college search process will turn out well. This book is an effort to help the parents of middle school students understand the basic facets of the college admissions process. It is important that parents develop a sense of confidence so that when the time comes for their children to begin the college search, they will know what to do, what to look for, and how to support them during this important family effort.

Although it will be the child who goes off to college, the best college searches are the result of a family endeavor. It is essential for parents to play a key role in the college search and application process. It is also necessary to trust in the skills and qualities they've instilled and nurtured in their children and let them work their way through this challenging, yet exciting process. Although the stakes may seem too high to let a child make these decisions for himself, he has been well prepared by you. If it helps, parents should try to remember his first steps—how it felt and the look on his face when he realized he could do it. You had to get over the fear that he would hit his head on the coffee table or fall squarely on his bottom. He probably did both of those things many times, but he got up, got better, and gained confidence in himself. Imagine the confidence he'll gain when he realizes he got himself into college and where that confidence will take him, especially when the stakes are so high.

This book is about helping parents make good decisions about their children's middle school and early high school years so that when the time comes for them to share the decision making with their children, everyone is confident and well prepared.

Chapter 1

College Admissions
The Basics

Every year thousands of students from outside the United States flock to this country to pursue university-level study. These students come from many countries and, while their individual reasons for making this journey vary, one common reason they choose to attend American colleges and universities is for the variety of higher education options available here. Fortunately, American students don't need to obtain visas and cross borders to have access to a wealth of college choices.

The benefit of so many college options is obvious: There is a college to fit every type of student and any kind of interest and goal. The disadvantage, however, may not be as clear. With so many choices, students and families need to know what they want just to zero in on the type of college that is right for them; finding the individual school that suits their needs requires significant time, effort, and self-awareness. While the tendency in such a situation might be to start considering college options early, so that one can weed out those that are not appealing, it is best to resist this temptation. Beginning a formal college search during the junior year of high school is early enough to consider all the factors one may feel are important and is the correct time developmentally and logistically to do so. Families who begin the college search prior to about the middle of eleventh grade risk making decisions based on incomplete academic information and interests and needs that may be immature. Additionally, while the college search can be an exciting and meaningful family adventure, most students and parents agree that about 18 months devoted to it is long enough!

An Embarrassment of Riches

In so many areas, America enjoys an embarrassment of riches, and college options is one such area. Whether a student wants to become a fire fighter and eventually an arson investigator, or wants to study the intricacies of quantum physics, a college exists to develop these interests. In fact, chances are there are more than one. There are over 3,000 colleges and universities across the United States. They are located in each state, in urban, rural, and suburban settings, and they enroll anywhere from a few hundred students to tens of thousands of undergraduates. Additionally, colleges have distinct personalities and institutional philosophies that influence and drive the undergraduate experience. In America, unlike in other parts of the world, students consider many factors when deciding where to go to college. In other countries, students will enroll at the university that is closest to their home or that offers the "best" academic program in their area of interest. While location and academic program are key factors in an American college search, other considerations come into play as well, such as the setting, the size of the student body, and the culture on campus.

Whether our children are seeking advice about whom to ask to their first dance or what to do with their lives, as parents it is our role to provide guidance for them. In order to be able to give the best advice, it is important to be aware of the options available. This can be difficult, especially if your own educational opportunities were limited by geography, finances, or lack of exposure.

Distinguishing Qualities

At the most basic level there are two qualities that distinguish colleges and universities: their source of funding and the type of degree granted. Colleges are either public or private—public institutions receive a majority of their funding from state and federal government sources, while private institutions must rely on their own endowments and private contributions for funds. While both types of institutions garner funding from public and private sources, in addition to tuition revenue, the majority of their operating budget comes from one type of source. The source of a university's funding can impact the activities of the institution, which may be a consideration for prospective students. Fiscal difficulties at the state or federal level, caused by a weak economy, for example, can limit the funding available for faculty salaries or student programs. As a result, class sizes could increase or student activities could be limited. Of course, financial problems are not limited to public institutions; private colleges can have their share of challenges also.

The length of time it takes to earn the degree granted by the school determines whether it is a two-year or a four-year institution. Two-year colleges grant associate degrees, while students at four-year colleges and universities earn bachelor's degrees. Four-year colleges may also have graduate divisions that offer advanced degrees—master's and doctoral degrees. Typically, "colleges" award only bachelor's degrees, while "universities" can bestow master's and doctoral degrees as well. There are, of course, exceptions to this rule and well-known "colleges," such as Dartmouth College in New Hampshire, offer MBA and medical degrees. Generally, though, most "colleges" focus on undergraduates, while "universities" offer both undergraduate and graduate programs.

Other Categories

Beyond these basic characteristics, colleges fall into other, broader categories. The academic offerings available at the school dictate into which category it falls: There are public and private schools that fall into each. Although schools can be categorized as one type of institution, the college or university may, in fact, possess characteristics of one or more of the other types of schools. A large research university, for example, may be "comprehensive" in that it offers a college with a liberal arts focus, and another that emphasizes engineering. The overall nature of the school, however, is research based. Below are the most common types of American colleges along with examples of each.

Liberal Arts Colleges

Liberal arts colleges, despite the use of the term "college," come in all shapes and sizes. The hallmark of a liberal arts institution is its curriculum. While the range of majors offered may be expansive, at the core of the academic experience at a liberal arts school is the mission to instill in students an understanding and appreciation of the traditional arts and sciences. Students ultimately choose to focus their studies in one field such as economics or physics, but at least some portion of their undergraduate years will be devoted to gaining broad exposure in a range of subjects, often including English, history, social science, math, science, foreign language, and the arts. The goal is to instill variety while affording depth through the selection of the major.

Some schools offer a "core curriculum," a standard set of courses that students must take in order to graduate. The philosophy behind a core curriculum is that it is important for all students to share a common intellectual foundation as it will serve as a basis for all additional studies. A core curriculum generally also emphasizes the tenets of Western civilization, believing they are the foundation of a high caliber, well-rounded education. Columbia College, the undergraduate liberal arts school of Columbia University in New York City, is an example of a school that has a core curriculum in place. The program requires a sequence of courses that includes a full year of Contemporary Civilization designed to "introduce students to a range of issues concerning the kinds of communities—political, social, moral, and religious—that human beings construct for themselves and the values that inform and define such communities" (Columbia University web site, 2003), in addition to five courses devoted to the study of humanities through a survey of Western literature, philosophy, art, and music. There are other distribution requirements in addition to the core curriculum in areas such as language, non-Western culture, and physical education. Other schools take a more flexible approach and allow students to select classes from different proscribed areas of study. Kenyon

College, a private liberal arts college in Gambier, Ohio, is an ideal example of a school that employs a flexible distribution requirement system for its undergraduates. Kenyon provides "diversification guidelines" that allow "students to gain experience in all four academic divisions: the fine arts, humanities, natural sciences, and social sciences. The aim is to insist on variety and avoid premature specialization. Also, because the guidelines are liberal, they encourage curiosity and experimentation" (Kenyon College web site, 2003). In addition to courses in the four areas above, students must also fulfill requirements in foreign language and quantitative reasoning.

Regardless of what the requirements are, generally, they can be completed early in a student's college career, usually within the first two years. Students then move on to their major course of study and electives in other areas of interest. In addition to the course of study required of students, another distinguishing feature of liberal arts schools is the emphasis on the undergraduate experience. Although some liberal arts institutions offer graduate degrees, undergraduate students receive significant faculty attention and guidance, unlike schools that focus on graduate programs and faculty research, which bring in attractive and extensive government funding.

Research Universities

As the name implies, institutions that are categorized as "research universities" emphasize research at all levels. Although not exclusively, research universities tend to be large. Faculty tenure decisions are based upon the quality, prominence, and, to some degree, quantity of research. Because research is so important, students as assistants are equally important, as they provide much-needed support for research projects and grants. Fortunately for graduate students, research positions are often accompanied by stipends and other educational and/or residential perks. What is good for graduate students, however, is sometimes not so good for undergraduates. Graduate students, not undergrads, may receive priority for equipment use and faculty resources. While graduate students will often be the main beneficiaries of research opportunities at these institutions, undergraduates may also be able to take part. Participating in a research project as an undergraduate can be very rewarding and especially beneficial to future graduate school or career plans, and students should be encouraged to investigate any opportunities during their college years.

Another feature of research universities with an abundance of graduate assistants is the "teaching assistant." Because some may measure the quality of a university by the percentage of full-time faculty and how many have a Ph.D. or the terminal degree in their field, they may believe that teaching assistants are not the best-qualified teachers. To the contrary, graduate students don't have the same pressure to publish that tenure-track faculty do and, because they are still entrenched in their own studies, they may be more on the cutting edge of their field, making them quite up-to-date and appealing teachers. The University of Pittsburgh in Pennsylvania is a prime example of a research institution. While it offers a broad range of courses and students can obtain an education similar to that of a liberal arts college with regard to breadth of study, the university receives significant funding in the form of research grants and devotes considerable resources, human and financial, to research efforts, distinguishing it as a research university.

Specialized Schools

Specialized schools are institutions that offer a highly focused course of study. While other fields may be represented in the curriculum, they may be offered only at an introductory or cursory level. Within this category would be conservatories and technical, business, and health science schools. Students choosing one of these types of schools must have a clear and well-founded desire to pursue such a limited course of study. Although younger children may be exhibiting affinities for certain areas, such as the arts or science, it is probably too early to seriously consider a specialized school when a child is in middle school. It may be helpful, though, to know what these schools are and their strengths if your child has shown a great deal of talent and interest in a specific field. If your child's talents and passion for a field do continue to grow throughout adolescence, it is very beneficial to understand the requirements of specialized programs, especially conservatory requirements, early in high school in order to be best prepared to meet the audition and portfolio guidelines used for admission purposes.

Technical Schools

Although technical schools often have programs in nontechnical fields, their focus is on the sciences, engineering, computer science, and other high-tech areas. Often, programs are very hands-on, providing substantial experiential-based educational opportunities. While those categorized as technical schools can certainly offer programs outside the realm of science and technology, such offerings are not generally substantial. Nor do these schools have a reputation in these non-technical areas. Rensselaer Polytechnic Institute in Troy, New York, exemplifies a technical school. It has a tremendous number of major programs with most, if not all, related to science and technology. Programs with a link to the humanities even have a more technological feel with titles such as "Electronic Media, Arts, and Communication" and "Language, Literature, and Communication" (Rensselaer Polytechnic Institute web site, 2003).

Conservatories

Conservatories can be free-standing institutions or part of larger colleges or universities that offer a broader academic program. Conservatory programs offer specialized training in the arts and generally require some sort of audition or adjudication as part of the admission process. Students will most likely have limited, if any, requirements outside their chosen field of study unless they choose to participate in a dual-degree program with a cooperating institution or another division within the larger university setting of which the conservatory is a part. The Juilliard School in New

York City is a well-known example of a free-standing conservatory. The school has cooperative agreements with other institutions, such as Columbia University, but in order to take courses at both, students must apply to and be admitted by both schools. Students who graduate from Juilliard earn a Juilliard degree. Oberlin College Conservatory of Music in Ohio is the oldest continuously operating conservatory of music in the United States. The conservatory has been part of Oberlin College since 1867, two years after it was founded as a private school (Oberlin College web site, 2003). Today, students interested in pursuing a course of study broader than music must also apply to the arts and science division of Oberlin, but both programs are part of the same institution.

Comprehensive Colleges and Universities

Offering the same breadth of academic programs as a liberal arts institution along with the focused programs of a specialized school, comprehensive colleges and universities are able to provide the best of both worlds. At comprehensive institutions, while there might be different undergraduate divisions, there are no distinct schools, meaning that all students at the college or university are required to meet the same or quite similar requirements for graduation. They also have access to courses throughout all academic disciplines. These schools differ from universities that offer separate colleges of engineering, liberal arts, fine arts, and others, each with its own graduation requirements, as cross-registration between distinct colleges may also be limited. Institutions such as Lafayette College in Easton, Pennsylvania, offer broad liberal arts curricula as well as established and highly regarded engineering programs, illustrating the offerings of a comprehensive college.

Single-Sex Colleges

Although only a relatively few colleges of this type remain, they are an important part of American higher education. Most of the nation's earliest colleges were single-sex and served only young, white, affluent males—

in fact, using the term "single-sex" to describe early American colleges would likely have been redundant. Women's colleges developed over the years and were initially the only option females had for higher education. Most single-sex colleges fall into the liberal arts category of school, offering a broad, traditional curriculum. Bryn Mawr College in Bryn Mawr, Pennsylvania, is an example of an all-women's college and Hampden-Sydney College in Hampden-Sydney, Virginia, represents the all-male category. Despite challenges, often economic in nature, that prompted a number of formerly single-sex institutions such as Lehigh University and Vassar College to become coeducational, today's single-sex colleges remain steadfast in their commitment to educating either young men or young women, allowing each to fulfill their potential.

Historically Black Colleges and Universities (HBCUs)

Historically Black Colleges and Universities come in all types and sizes. While they do not formally restrict their enrollment to African-American students through their admission policies, a vast majority, if not all, of their students are. Although a number of American colleges and universities began admitting African-American students early in their histories, for many black students, HBCUs were the only choice available to them for decades. It has only been since the latter half of the twentieth century that African-American students have had broad access to colleges and universities as a result of an increase in recruitment and retention efforts designed to attract students of color. HBCUs are located throughout the country and offer all types of academic programs. Spelman College and Morehouse College, both located in Atlanta, Georgia, are selective, high-profile Historically Black Colleges that attract and enroll academically strong African-American students.

Service Academies

Four colleges in the United States incorporate the training of the country's military elite into their mission. The United States Military Academy

(USMA) or West Point, the United States Naval Academy (USNA) or Annapolis, the United States Air Force Academy (USAF), and the United States Coast Guard Academy are on the list of the nation's most competitive institutions and attract the best and brightest students the country has to offer. There is no monetary cost to the student to attend a service academy, but those who enroll make a commitment to military service upon graduation. Each campus is unique, reflecting their diverse locations. They offer a rigorous curriculum, demand self-discipline, and mold leaders. Each has its own rich sense of tradition and those who graduate become part of a close-knit community, bonded by a shared experience. Service academies are different from military schools such as The Citadel in South Carolina and Virginia Military Institute (VMI) in Virginia. These schools are privately operated institutions and, while they educate young men and, more recently, women, in military traditions, their graduates do not incur an obligation to enter the service.

Religiously Affiliated Colleges

Like single-sex and Historically Black Colleges, religiously affiliated schools take a variety of forms. As a group, they offer a broad range of academic programs in a variety of settings. There are colleges and universities affiliated with many religions. Prominent examples of religiously affiliated schools are Brigham Young University (the Church of the Latter-day Saints/Mormon Church), Provo, Utah, and Boston College (Jesuit/Roman Catholic Church), Boston, Massachusetts. While some schools have what is referred to as an historical tie to a specific church, which means that while the organization was instrumental in the college's founding, it is no longer an influential force on the campus or the student body. Schools that still claim an official tie to a specific religion are largely influenced by it and its tenets. At a Roman Catholic college, for instance, a pro-choice student organization is not likely to receive institutional funding for its activities if such a group exists at all. Religiously affiliated schools may also have graduation requirements linked to the church so it is important to understand the nature of the affiliation before choosing to enroll at this type of school. In some cases, religiously affiliated schools may give preference in their admission process to students of that faith but many remain open to enrolling students from all backgrounds and to meeting their spiritual needs once on campus. Georgetown University in Washington, D.C., the nation's oldest Catholic Jesuit institution, for instance, was one of the first colleges in the United States to employ a full-time rabbi on campus to serve the needs of its Jewish student population and broaden the religious perspective on campus as a whole.

Community Colleges/Junior Colleges

These schools offer two-year academic programs and are designed to provide either academic preparation for students planning to transfer to a four-year institution or preparation for certain career fields that may require some advanced education but not a four-year degree. In some cases, students who need academic remediation will choose a two-year school in order to strengthen the skills needed to succeed in a four-year program. There are community colleges in most counties or regions in the United States; they are supported by local funds and offer open admission policies and reasonable tuition, thereby serving all residents. Private two-year schools exist throughout the country and serve a range of students. Dean College in Franklin, Massachusetts, is an example of a junior college that is not publicly funded. While Dean offers one baccalaureate degree, a vast majority of its offerings are at the associate degree level. Many of Dean's graduates go on to four-year colleges to pursue a bachelor's degree.

Too Many Options: How to Choose

Sometimes, when faced with a lot of options, the natural tendency may be to start considering the choices immediately, sifting through alternatives blindly without any focus. Under these circumstances, you certainly will gather a significant amount of information, but much of it may be irrelevant and the exercise will most likely be time consuming. Certainly, finding the right college for your child is worth the time and effort but jumping directionless into a search for the educational Holy Grail is not the most efficient or effective use of it. When making any decision, it is important to define the question, determine what the desired outcome is, and understand the ramifications of the choice. Choosing a college is no different. As mentioned previously, beginning the college search too early will result in wasted effort as the factors to consider cannot be clearly defined or may be erroneous if the child is still too young to know what he wants. As parents know, the whims of a preteen or teen change often, if not daily. Knowing what will be important to an 18-year-old when he is 12 is impossible. What *is* possible, however, is understanding what general factors to consider in the college choice and keeping tabs on the student's interests over the course of the middle and early high school years.

Which Factors Are Important and Which Are Fluff?

Early in their college search, many students find it hard to identify their preferences and interests. Often, it seems, students have never really been given the opportunity to make serious decisions about their future and they are literally stymied by the prospect of making one. Certainly we don't ask our toddlers which car seat they prefer or query our preteens about which mutual funds to add to our portfolios, nor should we. As parents, however, we do need to allow our children to begin making appropriate and limited-scale decisions as youngsters.

In addition to being a little overwhelmed by the thought of making a decision about where to go to college, some students also have difficulty expressing any preferences at all. It may be that students' thoughts and ideas haven't been taken seriously in the past or, perhaps, haven't even been solicited. While it's certainly not appropriate to abdicate family decision making to our grade-schoolers, it may be helpful to include children in the discussions about issues involving the family that you believe to be suitable. Helping your child begin to understand the dynamics of making decisions in a safe, low-risk environment can help him make good choices later in life about college and other things that are even more important.

What to Consider

The most basic qualities to consider when starting to investigate college options are characteristics such as student body size, location, setting, campus type, academic offerings, and admissions criteria. As noted above, it is difficult and not advised to begin making specific college choices for children much before the middle of their high school years. First of all, children's preferences and interests can change dramatically from year to year, so beginning too early may cause an important decision to be made based on inaccurate information garnered from immature goals. Also, from an academic perspective, high school is a different world from elementary and middle school. Not that there aren't demanding teachers in children's early school years or that the concepts aren't difficult to grasp, but many view the elementary and middle school years as ones during which they develop, refine, and strengthen skills. Grading, as a result, may be more subjective, more general, and, perhaps, less stringent than in high school. It's easy for the parents of a kindergartener to believe that Harvard is an option when reviewing a report card full of "Os" for Outstanding; after all, their child must be at the head of the class. Grading, competition, and concepts, however, get tougher after kindergarten and while all children progress to the first grade, not every high school graduate moves on to the Ivy League. In fact, the nation's most competitive colleges and universities accept between 10 and 15 percent of their applicants, most of whom are more than qualified to attend. The point here is that until a student's high school academic record has some definition, it is essential that parents not zero in on specific schools because they may be way off base with regard to the reality of their child's future credentials.

Evaluating the important factors that go into making a college choice in a general sense, however, can be helpful. Some of the more generic, yet essential, factors to consider are: location, setting, type of campus, size of student body, cost, and admissions criteria. Because children may be uncertain of what their interests and needs are, it will be very helpful to survey many of the options in each category to see which resonates with the student as the college search begins.

Location

There are two areas over which parents often exert their influence in their child's college search—location and cost. Some students have no awareness of the cost of college and what that burden might mean to their parents; they don't really consider cost as a factor for them. Very few, however, are unaware of the importance of location in their college search. Parents, on the other hand, can really draw the line when it comes to location so it is very important to begin thinking about how much distance between you and your child you both can tolerate. Once the time comes to discuss college options with your child, it is important to be open and honest about your feelings so everyone knows what options are legitimate. Depending on where you live, location can be more or less a limiting factor. Certain parts of the country have higher concentrations of colleges and universities, making it easier for students who live in these areas to find colleges that meet their needs within close proximity of their home. Students who live in areas that offer fewer college choices may find that they must travel further to find an institution that meets their needs.

Setting

Some find the hustle and bustle of a city invigorating and motivating, while others find it distracting. The isolation of a rural location to some is stifling, while others find it ideal for reflection and self-awareness. Determining which is right for your child can direct the college search. Like the geographic location of a college, parents can exert significant influence over the type of setting their child's potential college choice is in. Some parents are very concerned about an urban location and the safety of their children in that type of environment. Whatever your feelings, it is important to know that there are dangers in every location and teaching children to behave safely by making good choices no matter where they go to college is essential. Colleges and universities are required by law to provide prospective and current students with campus crime statistics. When considering various college choices, be sure to ask the admissions office or the campus safety and security department for the school's safety statistics.

One setting unique to the college experience is "the college town." Epitomized by towns such as State College, Pennsylvania, home of Penn State University, and Blacksburg, Virginia, where Virginia Tech is nestled, the college town is a setting dominated by the university where a majority of the population is college-aged or near to it and the businesses and establishments cater to them. College towns are generally somewhat isolated but few students are concerned by this circumstance as their needs, intellectual, social, and recreational, are well met.

Type of Campus

As with setting, the kind of campus one finds appealing can vary tremendously from student to student. Some like the interaction with the "real world" provided by a university that is integrated into its surrounding location, such as George Washington University in Washington, D.C. Others love the security and peacefulness of a contained campus that gives definition to the college community, such as Drew University's beautifully wooded campus in Madison, New Jersey, a bedroom community of New York City. There are advantages to both types of campuses and what is most comfortable to a student will be best.

Size of Student Body

While college guidebooks will offer parameters for somewhat commonly accepted student body sizes at colleges categorized as small, medium, large, and extra large, the size of the student body, more than almost any other characteristic, is relative. A student, for example, who was part of a high school graduating class of 700 students will likely find a college of 2,000 undergraduates quite small. A student who graduates from a high school with fewer than 100 classmates, however, may find a college of 2,000 quite large. Because of the relative nature of the student body size, it is very important for families to visit a range of colleges and decide what feels most comfortable.

Cost

Your financial circumstances will dictate how much the price of a college education will factor into your child's college search. Certainly, with the cost of most colleges today, even the most affluent of families must consider, on some level, the financial commitment of higher education. Financing a college education is the topic of a subsequent chapter, but it is important to note here that as with other considerations in the college search, it is best for families to have an open, frank discussion about any financial limitations prior to beginning the search. It will also be helpful to seek assistance from financial aid professionals to be certain that all forms of aid are considered.

Other Factors

As your child's individual interests and aspirations come into focus, it will be important to determine what other factors might influence the college search. For example, a student with an interest and strength in drama will obviously want to consider the theater facilities on campus. What may be less obvious is that you should also ask about performance opportunities as some colleges may limit roles to students who have chosen to major in theater. Depending on which side of the decision to major in theater or not your child is on determines whether such a restriction is an advantage or disadvantage. Parents of younger children should keep tabs on their children's interests and goals to begin determining what specific qualities should make the final list of college characteristics they and you want to consider.

After the College Search: The Admissions Office Decides

Despite the information often shared at cocktail parties and on the sidelines of soccer games by participants or veterans of the college search, college admission decisions are thoughtful, often heart-wrenching choices. Today's admissions officers read hundreds or thousands of applications each year, poring over student files, making decisions that they know will shape the future of these individuals. These decisions are based upon both objective and subjective information provided by students and high school personnel. The most important thing to remember when trying to understand how admissions decisions are made is that admissions officers are looking for trends and patterns within the student's credentials. Consistently strong academic performance in a rigorous program or an improving record are likely to be viewed favorably by admissions officers; a decline in grades or weak performance throughout high school create a less competitive portfolio.

The High School Record

Ask virtually any admissions officer and he or she will tell you that the single most important factor in a student's application is the high school record. The high school record is the complement of courses students complete during high school and their academic performance in those classes. When considering the high school record of an applicant, admissions officers must also consider the strength of the student's high school. Admissions officers spend a great deal of time familiarizing themselves with high school programs and curricula. High schools aid this process by providing a school profile that is submitted with each application. The profile includes information about the high school, its offerings, and the students who attend. Often included in the profile is information about the courses available and the level at which they are offered, such as honors, Advanced Placement (AP), or International Baccalaureate (IB). Some admissions officers will review a student's transcript with the high school profile nearby, checking off the honors, AP, or IB courses the student has taken. It is essential, therefore, that as a parent you educate yourself about the options available at the high school your child will attend and take an active role in determining which courses are good choices for him.

Tests

Tests are a fact of life. College admissions is no different and, certainly, the use of tests in the process is more pronounced than in most other areas. A discussion of the standardized tests used in college admissions follows but it is important to note here that studies have shown that when standardized tests are used in conjunction with a student's high school record, they are good predictors of college success. This is not to say that a student with modest test scores will not gain admission to a "good" college or that a student with high test scores is destined with certainty to gain admission to a prestigious college. Rather, parents and students must understand that standardized tests are important in college admission and coming to grips with that reality will affect the college search in a positive way by allowing families to focus on appealing and appropriate college choices.

Extracurricular Activities

A student's extracurricular profile indicates to an admissions office what that student is likely to contribute to the school's campus life. While the main consideration when making admissions decisions must be on whether or not students are capable of succeeding academically at the college, how students might be involved on campus and how they add to the residential life of the school are important as well. At today's most competitive colleges, where so many students in the applicant pool are capable of academic success, the extracurricular profile of a student may, in fact, tip the scales in favor of one over another.

A common concern of parents is that certain activities are valued more than others. This is simply not the case and even if it was, trying to pinpoint which activity an admissions officer at a specific school will find appealing at the time your current 12-year-old will be enrolling in college is impossible. What college admissions officers want to see are students who have actively participated in their schools, communities, and families, and who have developed and committed to personal interests and goals, no matter what they are. After all, colleges and universities are communities, and it is important to rejuvenate and sustain the traditions and unique features that distinguish a school, and only students who become invested in it will be able to do that. Remember, too, employment or family responsibilities, such as caring for a younger sibling or older family member, are also valuable experiences and may limit how much time a child can devote to traditional extracurricular activities. Again, such involvement is not better or worse than another. It is different and shows a high level of responsibility and maturity. No matter what your family situation requires or allows, encouraging children to get out from behind the controls of the X-Box and get involved in the world around them is an important role as a parent.

Recommendations

Recommendations are part of many selection processes. On our résumés as adults we either include the names and contact information of professional and/or personal references or indicate that this information is available on demand. Admissions officers find the information provided by someone familiar with a candidate's strengths, weaknesses, and character beneficial when deciding whether or not the candidate will be a welcome addition to the college community.

Many colleges and universities require a reference from a school official as part of their application process. A recommendation from a student's guidance or college counselor and/or a teacher or two may be requested. If teacher recommendations are required, families should carefully consider whom to ask. A teacher who can describe a student's work ethic and intellectual growth and include commentary on the child as a person, not just as a student, is a great choice. In some cases, such a teacher may not necessarily be the teacher in whose course a student earned an A, although that is always a plus!

Essays or Personal Statements

Some, but not all, colleges require an essay or personal statement as part of the formal application process. There are dozens of resources available when it comes time to write the college essay and although the topic of the essay is not likely to come to light until your child is a high school junior or senior, the experiences he is having in middle school may impact the ultimate choice of topic. As with extracurricular activities, some parents fall victim to the idea that there is some perfect essay or essay topic that families must find before the student applies to college. Again, this notion is false. It is important to remember that college applicants are merely high school seniors with only 17 or 18 years of life experience behind them. Some are fortunate to have had incredible experiences within that time frame, while others become compelling candidates because of the tragedies and obstacles they have overcome. In truth, however, most applicants to college have led pretty ordinary lives, and yet many are able to write descriptive, informative college essays that accomplish their goal, helping an admissions officer assess the student's writing skills and gain an understanding of the student beyond the academic credentials in the application. When it is time for your child to write a college essay, remember, the essay is about his experience and the best essays are not the overpolished, overedited documents that come from a high-priced consulting group, an overly helpful English teacher, or even a parent. As scary as it may be, let your child take ownership of the essay; it and the application as a whole will be stronger as a result.

Interviews

Some colleges and universities offer or require an interview with an admissions officer as part of the application process. Other schools, not having the admissions staff needed to meet the demand for interviews, will enlist the assistance of alumni in their interviewing efforts. Generally, it is a good idea to take advantage of an interview if one is offered. Although preparing for an interview of any kind can be nerve-racking, what prospective college students must remember is that the admissions interview is used as a forum to learn about the student's interests, goals for college and beyond, and high school experiences. Students should be prepared, as obvious as it sounds, to talk about themselves and what is important to them. In addition to thinking about what they want from the college experience when preparing for the interview, students should also investigate the school with which they are interviewing in order to develop a list of questions pertinent to their interests. Even well before the time for college admissions interviews, parents can help their children prepare for this eventuality by encouraging the development of strong social skills. Modeling good social skills, such as maintaining strong eye contact, offering a firm handshake, and holding balanced and engaging conversations, can help students tremendously in the college search and, more importantly, in life.

The College Search: A Language All Its Own

Like any specialized field, college admissions has its own language. As you begin, some terms may be very unfamiliar, making an already challenging exercise confusing. Taking the time to learn some of the lingo will be helpful to you and your child, as you can understand what you read and hear from the admissions experts you will encounter. A full Glossary of Terms has been included at the end of this book, but following are some essential terms that will prove useful in understanding college admissions.

The College Board

The College Board is a membership organization for college and secondary school professionals who work in the field of college admissions counseling. This organization administers the SAT I, SAT II, and PSAT.

Early Action (EA)

A nonbinding admissions plan under which a student will receive an admissions decision after a short period of time but is not required to enroll if admitted.

Early Decision (ED)

A binding admissions plan under which a student who agrees to enroll at a specific college if offered admission will be notified of his admission decision in a short period of time, generally several weeks or a month.

Educational Testing Service (ETS)

The organization that develops and designs the SAT.

Extracurricular Profile

The activities a student pursues outside of school make up his extracurricular profile. The profile includes any athletic, artistic, personal interests, employment, or community service endeavors to which a student commits his time. These activities are then listed on a student's application for admission to college.

High School Record

A student's high school record is usually the most important component in a college application. The term refers to the student's course of study, including the type and level of courses taken, as well as how the student has performed.

Regular Decision

The admissions program most commonly offered by colleges. Despite the popularity of Early Decision or Early Action programs, most students still apply to college under Regular Decision programs. These programs require students to apply for admission by a specific date. All applicants are then notified of their admissions decisions at the same time, generally in mid-spring.

Rolling Decision

An admissions decision program under which colleges and universities will determine a final admissions decision as an application becomes complete. Students are notified of the decision on a "rolling" basis.

Standardized Testing

Refers to the nationally normed and standard format tests that students generally must complete in order to apply for admission to college. The three tests commonly required for college admission are the SAT I, the SAT II, and the ACT.

QUESTIONS TO ASK

- What kind of learning environment, such as large or small classroom setting, seems likely to be best suited to my child's learning style?
- Are there talents or interests my child possesses that seem untapped?
- What opportunities are there for my child to strengthen his or her writing skills?
- Does the school encourage the development of good social and public speaking skills? Is my child progressing well in these areas?

A CHECKLIST FOR AN EFFECTIVE COLLEGE SEARCH

❑ Encourage your child's interests and keep current with them.

❑ Model good reading habits.

❑ Develop a financial plan, in consultation with a financial planning professional, to meet or ameliorate college costs.

❑ Create opportunities for your child to make or participate in making decisions in a safe, low-risk setting.

Chapter 2

Academic Planning
The Early Years

I
t seems that we begin to track, whether our schools call it that or not, our children's academic progress as soon as they bring home their first report card. The proportion of Os for Outstanding on the report card or the reading group to which our children are assigned are of great importance to us and seem to dictate our children's success later in their educational career. Never mind that the Os are for things such as "Plays well with others" or "Cleans up her area after snack." Or maybe these personal skills are, in fact, important indicators for lifelong success after all. Certainly, the ability to relate to one's peers and to determine how to meet the expectations of those in authority are skills that can bring significant approval and success. Whether we deem these skills valuable or not, as parents we are still concerned with the academic performance of our children and what it may mean to their future. Once the days of Os and reading groups are behind them, however, the standard for success as well as the stakes are much higher, or at least they seem to be. What becomes important is how our children are "positioned" and what more can we do to help them "get ahead."

When considering how to best help our children in their academic life, it is imperative to remember that each child has different strengths and weaknesses. Not all children are good at all things, nor should they be expected or forced to be. In many forums, "playing to one's strengths" is a good strategy; the same is true in academic planning. While it is beneficial to identify strengths and to make decisions regarding course selection based on those strengths, it is essential to provide children with the means to develop a balanced academic portfolio; strengths can be enhanced through enrichment or acceleration but weaknesses should be examined as well. The middle school years provide a terrific opportunity to identify strengths while fostering improvement in areas of weakness. Unlike high school when a student's full record of achievement is reviewed before the student is allowed to move on to the next level, middle school is a time when students can take whatever steps are needed and appropriate to develop the strongest academic foundation possible.

The End Result: What Should Students Strive for Before High School?

Obviously, where we start has an impact on where we finish. All things being equal, if two people start a race with the same abilities and the same finish line ahead, but one is a few steps ahead of the other at the starting line, the one who begins in front will most likely stay in the lead. The same is true in the race toward college. Students who begin high school in higher-level classes will finish high school having completed more advanced courses and, as a result, will be better prepared; these students will most likely have a broader range of college options as well. While students and families do not always have curricular choices to make in middle school, as the curriculum is often prescribed by school, county, or state requirements, it is helpful to know what to look for and, should options be available, know which are most beneficial.

High School Requirements

Having an understanding of what colleges expect students to complete during high school is helpful as families ponder the academic program of the middle school years. Generally (and you will find yourself tired of hearing the phrase "it varies from college to college"), colleges and universities require four years of English and two to three years of math, history, science, and language. In many cases, it is extremely beneficial to exceed minimum requirements as students who have completed more than the bare minimum are not only more competitive applicants to college, they are better prepared.

Requirements Before High School

- In order to begin the journey toward college at the most advantageous point, students must achieve a certain status before starting high school. Paramount to academic success in many areas is the ability to communicate clearly, correctly, and effectively. A student, therefore, should focus significant effort on developing strong writing skills. No matter what area a student chooses to focus on later in life, being able to write well will increase her likelihood for further and greater success. Fostering strong reading skills, and learning to be a critical and active reader, will also benefit the student tremendously, no matter what field she enters. Although facility with higher-level skills such as analytical and critical reading is beneficial, a solid foundation in the basics of writing, including grammar and syntax, is required for future academic success. Programs emphasizing the development of a broad active vocabulary should be considered beneficial as well.
- Students should be encouraged to enroll in the language arts and English courses that will provide them with the broadest yet strongest foundation in these fields as possible.
- In addition to taking advantage of the academic program available at their school, you should also encourage your children to read broadly and in excess of the school's curriculum. Such "outside" reading further develops the critical reading skills being fostered in the classroom and increases the vocabulary even more; the results of this relatively easy activity will likely be far-reaching.
- Social studies courses, including history and geography courses, are also at the core of a strong middle school curriculum. Although most high schools require significant history coursework for graduation,

many assume a proficiency in certain areas. For example, students should strive for a solid foundation in geography, a course not generally offered at the high school level but one that will provide a student with a certain knowledge base helpful in achieving success in future history courses. Students with a firm understanding of the different regions and major cultures of the world can focus on comprehending the "hows" and "whys" of historical events and synthesizing the information to draw insightful and sophisticated conclusions. Again, this level of achievement will allow the student to excel and progress further through the curriculum presenting the strongest possible academic program upon application to college.

- While placement in and the results of humanities courses is quite subjective, the outcomes of math and science courses are much less so. Students must master certain skills before moving on to more advanced courses and concepts. Studies have shown that completion of Algebra I and Geometry in eighth and ninth grades increases the likelihood of college enrollment and has a positive impact on the standardized test scores required for college admission. Additionally, if a student is to realistically aspire to enrollment in calculus as a senior in high school or before, he must complete Algebra I and possess a strong foundation in the course by the end of eighth grade. While enrollment in calculus is not necessarily a required component for a successful college search, it does enhance a student's academic portfolio significantly and provides strong preparation for the first year of college when students who have not completed calculus are encountering the difficult subject for the first time. Students with prior exposure to the subject are much more likely to achieve success.

- Among the most impressive qualifications a student can present as part of a college application is enrollment in a school's highest-level science courses. There are different philosophies regarding the order in which different fields of science are introduced in high school, but the most traditional offerings begin with biology and progress through chemistry to physics. Students who complete this sequence may then proceed to advanced levels in any of the subjects of particular interest to them. Some students may even choose to double up in science producing an even more impressive academic record. Upon the completion of middle school, a student should strive to have the scientific foundation to begin high school in the course that will allow her to complete the biology, chemistry, physics sequence (regardless of the order prescribed by her school) within three years so she can move on to higher-level study in the field.

- The study of foreign language is another area in which a student can distinguish herself in the college application process. While most of the nation's colleges require some language study in order to qualify for admission, the level of study expected is generally rather low. Even the nation's most selective colleges often view three years of language study as sufficient for admission, but students who exceed this level are certainly stronger applicants. If the student has access to foreign language classes in middle school, she should be encouraged to enroll in them as early as possible and to continue with the study throughout the high school years. Students who choose to study two foreign languages are few and far between and, therefore, even more distinctive in the college application process. Electing a program that includes two foreign languages, however, will most likely require a student to choose to eliminate study in a different area. Such a decision may, in fact, be a good one depending on the student's individual interests and strengths, but it may also be a poor choice. Again, the family must consider the full range of options and programs before making a final decision.

- In addition to courses in those areas we most often think of as needed for success in high school and college, many find exposure to the arts appealing. Study after study has shown that students who study music find their mathematical abilities enhanced. Even something as minimal (and easy) as listening to classical music prior to taking math tests has been shown to improve student scores on those exercises. Additionally, exposure to the arts increases the likelihood that students will tap into talents that may otherwise go undeveloped. Commitment to and achievement in the arts is often an appealing characteristic to present in the college application process.

Academic Planning and College Admissions

Although all college admission decisions are based on many factors, as you can imagine for all of the reasons noted above, a student's academic credentials remain the most important features in a college application. These credentials include more than just standardized test scores. In fact, the student's transcript, her high school record, is routinely noted by college admissions officers as the single most important component in an application. In addition to the student's performance in her classes, the high school record is the complement of courses she has taken, the level of rigor represented by this coursework, and any trends, either up or down, in her grades. All of these factors, illustrated clearly and in black and white, on the student's transcript will influence tremendously the outcome of a student's college search and application process.

Because of the importance of the high school transcript in the college application process, it is necessary to plan carefully in middle school to prepare a student to have access to the most challenging courses appropriate for her interests and abilities in her high school years. The courses a student takes in middle school and how she performs in them will determine what courses she will be advised and/or allowed to take in high school. As college admission becomes more competitive, the level of rigor in a student's course schedule, often measured by the number of honors and Advanced Placement (AP) or International Baccalaureate (IB) courses taken, has become increasingly more important. A student who performs poorly in middle school and the early high school years or who has not taken the proper prerequisite courses, no matter what her innate intellectual ability, will most likely not have access to her school's most challenging course offerings.

The Options Available

Each high school provides a range of academic offerings. It is important for families to be aware of the different kinds of courses available and to know what the requirements and prerequisites for enrollment in any of them are. As some states and/or schools have unique academic programs or types of diploma offerings, a family's best source of information regarding courses and course selection for the student will be the student's guidance counselor or academic advisor. Below is a list of the types of courses generally available in high schools.

Standard Courses

Standard-level high school courses are those offered by each high school that allow the student to achieve the academic proficiency needed to earn a high school diploma as determined by the state in which the student lives. These courses are available in all academic areas but do not provide the academic rigor of college preparatory or more advanced courses.

College Preparatory Courses

These courses are, by definition, designed to provide students with the academic groundwork necessary for college-level coursework. Generally available in all academic disciplines, students can acquire the broad, sound foundation necessary to achieve success in college. These courses will differ from standard-level courses in their breadth, depth, and workload expectations.

Honors Courses

Providing greater academic preparation by requiring students to move more quickly and with a greater depth of understanding, honors courses offer strong academic preparation for college, especially at the nation's most competitive institutions. Honors courses differ from other types of course offerings in that learning may be more student-initiated and teachers may expect more independent learning. A greater volume of work reflecting a greater level of understanding is often required for academic success in honors courses.

Advanced Placement (AP) Courses

Working through a curriculum developed by the College Board, students enrolled in AP courses move quickly through subject matter developing critical thinking and analytical skills, while preparing for an end-of-the-year exam. This standardized test, administered in May, affords the student the opportunity to earn college-level credit. Scored on a scale of 1 to 5, with 5 as the highest score, a student who earns 3 or higher may earn credit at the college at which she ultimately enrolls. Although some schools will award credit for scores of 3 or higher, most of the nation's more selective colleges will grant credit only for scores of 4 or 5. Additionally, while many schools will award academic credit for the results of the AP exam, some will grant credit toward graduation but will not exempt students from specific courses. In other words, the credit awarded will allow a student to complete the credit requirements for graduation more quickly or by taking fewer courses once enrolled, but the student may still be required to complete all the courses specified by her chosen major or by the school's graduation requirements.

International Baccalaureate (IB) Courses

Developed by the International Baccalaureate Organization, the IB curriculum is viewed by many educators as the most advanced academic program available at the secondary level in the United States. The IB program consists of both intense courses as well as complementary programs that include the Theory of Knowledge course, the Extended Essay, and the Creativity, Action, Service component, which, if completed in total, allow the student to earn the prestigious International Baccalaureate Diploma. This diploma was designed to provide students in American schools with a diploma option similar in rigor and intensity to some of the secondary school degrees granted in European countries such as France and Germany. Earning the full IB diploma, however, is time consuming and demanding. Students who choose this option may feel limited in the other activities they can pursue, which may not be the best choice for all individuals. Like the AP program, the IB offers students the chance to earn college-level credit through their performance on a standardized exam taken at the completion of the course. There are two IB levels: Higher and Subsidiary; some colleges will have different requirements for awarding credit based upon the IB level completed by the student. Graded on a different scale than Advanced Placement exams, students generally must earn scores of 5, 6, or 7 on an IB exam to earn credit.

Which Is Better?

Americans always seem to want to know what is "better." We rank everything from the year's "Most Intriguing People" to the best cars. We shouldn't be surprised, therefore, when publications start to place academic institutions and programs into some sort of priority order. What we need to remember, however, is that "best" is a relative term. What is perfectly suited for one may be perfectly awful or inappropriate for another. Along these lines, it seems that parents often ask if AP Calculus is "better" than AP English. In the eyes of a college admissions officer, neither course is better than the other. These courses, however, prepare a student differently, which may make one a better choice than the other for a particular student. A student interested in pursuing an engineering degree, for instance, may find an AP Calculus class especially helpful as she embarks on the math- and science-intensive first-year curriculum required of engineering students. A student and her family must first ask what the goals of the student are and then plan the best course of action to achieve them.

If the Student Is Struggling

Not all students succeed in all areas and some students may experience significant difficulty in many areas. If a student is having academic difficulty in middle school, it is important to address the issue as soon as it is apparent. There are many things parents can do to help a child who is struggling. The first step is to speak candidly with the child's teachers and advisors. Zeroing in on specific difficulties and determining a specific course of action for support and, if necessary, remediation is the best approach.

If working with the child's teacher to develop a new learning strategy is not successful, it may be necessary to seek outside assistance such as a subject-specific tutor. There are many local and national tutoring services that provide excellent support and may also help students develop strong study skills that may aid in future courses providing additional long-term benefits. Families might also want to consider summer academic programs or camps that would allow the child to continue her studies in a specific field in a more casual and fun atmosphere, thereby preventing the knowledge gained during the school year from being lost, yet still allowing the child to have a break from the traditional school setting.

While it is important to take whatever steps possible to help a child succeed at the middle school level, it is also important to remember that children develop at different speeds. The child who may be less motivated academically or who may struggle more with concepts as a preteen may become more focused or able as she continues to mature and develop in high school. So, while it is important not to ignore any academic difficulties encountered by the child in middle school, it is also important not to make more of them than necessary. As a child's future is not determined by the number of Os on her kindergarten report card, neither is it framed by the grades she earns in middle school.

Making Individual Choices

When considering a child's academic schedule it is essential to consider more than just what impact it will have on her college search and application process. What is most important is how it will best meet the interests, ability, and needs of the student. It is not necessary for each student to take every AP course offered by her high school in order to gain admission to college. Students should strive to build a balanced academic course load that reflects their interests and strengths. Because it is impossible to predict the outcome of the college application process, especially many years before actually participating in it, it is important not to make a student's enrollment in a particular college the only goal of the high school years, let alone the middle school years. If all decisions regarding a student's courses and goals are made with college in mind, if the student changes her mind about her college or career path, those decisions may be for naught. It is important to value the high school years for the experience, growth, and development they inherently provide, not just as a stepping-stone to college.

It is also important to keep in mind that the student is still a child and that undue pressure is neither necessary nor desired. The pressures of being a teenager today are much more imposing than those of even just a decade or two ago. In response to the pressures they have witnessed in the students in their applicant pool in recent years, a number of admissions officers at Harvard University, including the Dean of Admissions, wrote a paper entitled "Time Out or Burn Out for the Next Generation?" in the winter of 2001. The narrative focuses on the increasing pressure placed on today's children to be successful and the often well-meaning but ill-conceived path to this achievement. The impetus for the Harvard paper is the belief by many in selective college admissions that "the pressures on today's students seem far more intense than those placed on previous generations." Students and parents fight for their child's placement in the highest-level courses available and for the prominent positions in activities and on teams believing they will bring success in the college search process. The

Harvard article prompts one to ask "at what cost" such success will come. While it is helpful to consider all of the factors included here when making choices regarding a student's academic choices, the most important thing to keep in mind is the student, her abilities, and her needs. Choices made with these factors in the foreground will always be sound decisions.

A Team Effort

No matter how sincere, all the parental support in the world will not bring academic success if the student herself is not motivated to succeed. It is important that children share the same goal of college as their parents and that they understand, although are not made anxious by, the importance of consistent academic preparation and achievement. Sharing your hopes and expectations for college with your child will help her begin to assimilate the idea into her own thoughts and plans for the future.

Exposing your child to the kinds of experiences college can provide and introducing her to the notion that a college education can have a tremendous impact on her future career options will prove especially helpful in making college appealing. Parents who have attended college can share their own experiences through pictures and anecdotes and by introducing their children to friends made during those years. Discussing with children the impact college has had on their lives, from a personal, professional, and economic perspective, will allow them to understand how higher education can affect them personally and directly. Parents who have not attended college can ask friends or relatives who have attended to share their experiences with the children.

Children in middle school still enjoy activities with their parents; parents who did not attend college can learn right alongside their child about the many options available, making the process truly a family affair. No matter what your background, in order for college to be securely in your child's future, in order for her to make the necessary academic effort to make attendance possible, she must be as committed as you are. Like anyone, kids who are excited about something will work hard to achieve it.

- What are my child's choices regarding course selection in middle school?
- Are there different levels of courses available based upon student ability at the middle school level?
- Who will advise me and my child regarding academic offerings?
- If necessary, what support services are available to a child with learning differences?
- Who do I contact if my child is having academic difficulty and what support services are offered by the school or local agencies to help her?
- What are the different curricular offerings (such as the AP or IB program) and college placement experiences of the local high schools in the area and, if appealing, is it possible for my child to attend a high school other than the one she would normally attend?

A CHECKLIST FOR ACADEMIC PLANNING

- ❏ Obtain information regarding courses currently available.
- ❏ Discuss options and placement with student's guidance counselor or academic advisor.
- ❏ Review options and discuss them as a family.
- ❏ Consider academic plan in conjunction with student's other activities and commitments.
- ❏ Consider future academic ramifications of available course options.
- ❏ Map academic plan in context of current offerings and those available at the high school level.

Chapter 3

Study Skills for Middle School Students

School systems define middle school differently but generally the middle school years are sixth through eighth grades. In some areas fifth grade might also be included. Whatever grades your school considers middle school, when your child enters it you will likely begin to focus more seriously on the results of his academic efforts, in other words, his grades. Not that the reports you received in elementary school weren't important; the grade reports of middle school just seem more relevant to future success.

It's easy for parents to understand that elementary school is a time for building foundations, as almost everything a child learns during this time is new and the initial steps of larger concepts. Even the grading scale used in elementary school implies that the learning process—learning how to learn—is more important than the actual outcome. The beginning of middle school and the introduction of letter grades, though, seems to bring new importance to student performance. Because what a child learns in middle school creates the foundation for what he is able to learn in high school, these years are critical in a child's education.

Subject matter, however, is not the only important feature on which to focus during middle school. It is imperative that middle school students learn content, but it is equally essential that they learn how to learn and how to study. Parents, in conjunction with their child's teacher, should monitor not only the child's performance but how well he is developing effective study habits and skills, for while the content acquired is very important, learning the skills necessary to continue learning at a higher level and being able to apply what he knows to other situations is what will allow him to find future success.

Homework

Most likely, homework time will not be your child's favorite time of day. The distractions of friends, siblings, TV, and toys are very real. If properly organized, though, it can be an effective exercise that will help him earn better grades and feel more confident. Although it is necessary to have a regular, monitored homework time each day, the timing, length, and homework site should be tailored to your child's temperament. Some children will want to come right home and dig into homework to get it done and out of the way. Others will need time to decompress after a day at school. Neither is right or better. Let your child's personality and other priorities be your guide when determining how and when he does his homework. Important to the success of homework time is the setting in which it is completed. Your child should have a clean, well lit, and organized space in which to do his homework. He should have all the supplies he needs and he should not have easy access to the things that distract him, such as video games, the phone, or TV.

For some parents, it would never occur to them to do their child's homework or projects. For others, however, "helping" with such assignments can cross the line and the result may be something the child isn't capable of. In such cases, parents are trying to help their child either by relieving a burden or to ensure a better grade. In either case, however, the child is not being well served. In the long run, children will benefit more by learning to plan their time well to accomplish large tasks and will gain confidence in their own abilities as a result. Sometimes, a parent who is attempting to help a child by taking over a project can actually hurt his self-esteem by indicating to the child that the parent doesn't believe in the child's abilities, a result no parent wants to produce. The parent who assumes responsibility for a child's work in an effort to help him earn a better grade is actually taking away the "practice" that will help assure success in formal test settings. Homework is the practice session of school. While homework is often assigned a grade, it usually carries less weight in the overall grading scheme of the course. Teachers design classes this way in order to allow homework to be a means of practice on which a child can afford to make mistakes from which he can learn. As in any setting, if a child has his practice session taken away or doesn't use it effectively, he will not be as well prepared for the real test. Parents must provide the proper support without stepping over the line and actually doing the assignments for their child, as hard as it may be to watch them occasionally falter.

Web Sites for Homework

For many of us, the days of helping our children with homework may end with the introduction of long division. Fortunately, as your child moves into higher grades, calculators are commonly used and the Internet has spawned many web sites devoted to homework help and research for school projects. Chances are if you can't recall the components of an atom's nucleus or the proper use of colons, you can find the answer with a quick Web search. Some prominent web sites for homework help and school research are:

1. Discovery School.com—*http://school.discovery.com/homeworkspot.com*
2. Fact Monster—*http://www.factmonster.com*
3. Homework Helper—*http://www.refdesk.com/homework.html*
4. What You Need to Know About—*http://www.about.com/homework/*

Organization

Educators agree, organization is key to academic success. Looking at our own desks, home offices, or briefcases, it is easy to understand just how hard it is to be organized. As hard as it is for adults, it is even harder for children. Let's face it, few children of any age like to clean up and keep their living space tidy, let alone their notebooks, lockers, or backpacks. It is essential, therefore, that parents step in and help their child to set up an organizational system and maintain it.

Notebooks

Individual teachers may have notebook and school supply requirements. In such cases, obviously the child must follow these rules, as many teachers incorporate notebook checks into their grading system. If your child's teacher does not offer specific notebook guidelines, it is important for you to determine what kind of system will work best for your child. Most study skills resources recommend that a student have a separate notebook, spiral or loose-leaf, for each subject. The individual notebooks allow a student to keep all his notes, assignments, and so on in one place, facilitating studying and homework. If a spiral notebook is used, it is helpful for it to have at least one pocket for handouts and returned quizzes and tests. Loose-leaf binders allow students to add worksheets and teacher handouts and intersperse reading notes with class notes and homework. The use of binders also allows a student to add notes and homework at a later time in the event that he doesn't have the notebook in class. If a child decides to use a binder, it is important that there be individual sections for each subject and, within each section, subsections for reading notes, class notes, and homework assignments.

Obviously, the only way a notebook will be helpful to a student's school work is if it is used. Include your child in the selection of his school supplies if possible so he can decide what color or which character to have on the front. Additionally, as obvious as it may sound, be sure to purchase items that will fit easily into your child's book bag and locker. A child who is embarrassed by the "uncool" logo on his notebook, or who struggles to get it in or out of his backpack, is less likely to use it correctly and well.

Note Taking

There are many methods for successful note taking. What works best for your child will be a method that is well matched to his writing ability, his learning style, and his age. It is unreasonable to expect a young child who must laboriously print whatever he writes to record virtually every word a teacher says. This note-taking method isn't likely to be possible for a younger child, and it is probably not the most effective method for anyone. Students must figure out what note-taking system is best for them, and there are some tips that educators endorse.

1. It is important to utilize abbreviations and symbols in order to write less and communicate more. Common symbols such as + or & for "and"; = for "equals" or "is"; and e.g. in place of "for example" can save valuable writing time while trying to follow important comments from the teacher. Using such shorthand and developing one's own system can enhance a student's ability to take complete and effective class notes.
2. Students must learn that it isn't necessary and probably not desirable to write down everything a teacher says. It is important for children to begin to learn what is essential and what is not. One thing students should always do, however, is write down whatever the teacher writes on the board. Chances are if the teacher has found it important enough to write out for the class, it is important to know. When something is obviously important, students should mark such items with a symbol such as a star, check mark, or arrow, or underline the topic.
3. Class notes should be set up the same way each day. Students should begin each class by placing the date in a prominent location. It is helpful to leave wide margins and spaces between topics in order to add information that might be missed or that is relevant to it from readings and other assignments.

There are many ways to take notes and it is important for a student to find the one that works best for him. If your child needs some help taking effective notes, there is a note-taking system that has been shown to be effective. It is called the Cornell System and is a clear, well-organized note-taking system. Landmark College, a school that caters to the needs of students with learning disabilities, has modified the program somewhat but the basic principles are the same and are helpful to those students with learning difficulties and those without. Although for some students, rewriting class notes may be an effective means of acquiring information, a key principle of the Cornell System is that it allows students to take effective notes in the most efficient manner. Utilizing this system should allow students to take notes only once, without revision.

- Under this system, a student must use a loose-leaf binder and may write on only one side of the paper during class.
- A wide left margin is drawn or preprinted paper with a large margin can be purchased. This column is used to note key words or phrases.
- All class notes are taken to the right of the margin.
- Notes should be taken in paragraph form, focusing on general ideas.
- Students should skip lines between ideas.
- After class, the student should write key ideas and comments to the left of the margin to help recall the lecture later.
- Covering up either column and recalling the hidden information will serve as a useful study system as well as a good note-taking method.
- The back of each sheet serves as a place to write questions about the material for review purposes, to add pictures, and to add a summary.

The Cornell System will not work for all students but may be helpful to your child. A short-term trial run may be a good idea.

Test-Taking Skills

As in many situations, good planning and organization are key to good test-taking skills. Studies have shown repeatedly that "cramming" the night before a test is not an effective way to truly learn material. Shorter periodic study sessions have proven to be more effective efforts in test preparation, not to mention less nerve-wracking and anxiety-producing.

In addition to actually learning the material a test will cover, there are other things a student can do to improve his test performance. First, and while it may seem obvious, it is essential for a student to know what the test will cover. Wasting time and energy studying concepts and facts not included in the material the test will cover is a mistake. Time spent studying information that will not be on the test obviously takes time away from reviewing the material that *will* be on it.

Know the Format

Before preparing for the test, it is important to know what format the exam will take. Studying for a multiple-choice test is different from studying for an essay exam. Chances are, a multiple-choice test will require studying more specific details, while an essay exam may allow for less recall of specifics but will require a student to be able to express himself in his own words. If a test is essay in format, it will be beneficial to practice writing about the topics the test will cover. Regardless of what the test format will be, parents can help their children by creating questions in the appropriate format and quizzing them. The more exposure to a test format and repeatedly recalling the information prior to the test will contribute to a student's success.

Know the Information Covered

Some tests will include information that will be necessary to complete test questions but does not need to be memorized. Well before test day, the student should find out from the teacher what formulas, theories, and so on will be on the test and whether or not they will be provided or can be brought by the student on a notes or formula sheet. On science tests, for example, sometimes a formula will be included so the student can focus on using the formula as opposed to just memorizing it. A student could needlessly spend many hours studying formulas or charts that will be provided on the test; this would be a waste of time and could be easily avoided.

Choose the Right Study Location

As is the case with homework, it is important to study in a location that is quiet, free of distraction, and generally comfortable. Comfort is important but students shouldn't be so comfortable that they fall asleep or lose concentration. The study location should be a moderate temperature, free of distracting noise, and well lit. It should be clean and organized as well. In some cases, it may be helpful for your child's study area to be in a common space such as the kitchen or dining room so you can monitor his progress and limit distraction.

Plan a Study Schedule

Finally, students should plan a study schedule allowing for separate study sessions for each chapter or unit on a test and a final review session of all sections. Repetition is important in studying and some students may find that writing and rewriting information or notes is a helpful study tool for them. Another study technique that can be useful is writing questions about the test material and answering those questions.

Time Management

While the thought of a sixth-grader toting around a Palm Pilot or a DayTimer is somewhat scary, it is a good idea to help children learn the benefits of time management and planning early. Helping your child develop a plan for long-term products can be especially helpful to him. For many people, adults and children alike, figuring out how to tackle a large project can be very difficult. Assisting and guiding your child as he determines the main components of a large assignment and helping him work out a schedule for completing each part is an important job of a parent. You can help your child determine how much time each section will take and help him actually meet his deadlines. Using a calendar will allow your child to visualize the project and understand the importance of making and meeting deadlines. Additionally, crossing dates and milestones accomplished off the calendar can be very motivating to children as they progress.

Good time management skills are important in daily activities as well as in longer-term projects. Helping your child determine a schedule for his own day that takes into account the things he must complete each day, including getting ready for school, travel to and from school, time spent in class, any sports, music, or activities, homework, household responsibilities, and time to relax, is essential. While all aspects of your child's life are important, it is very important to help him create a regular and effective homework period. Again, some kids will benefit from getting their homework done shortly after school, while others need time to unwind and relax after school before getting down to work. Neither situation is right or wrong; what is best depends on your child. If the schedule you work out doesn't seem to suit him, don't be afraid to change it until you find a system that works.

My Child Is Working Hard and It Isn't Enough—What Now?

Sometimes student and parent are doing everything possible to ensure success in school and yet it is not working. Discuss the child's school experience with his teacher and determine the best course of action. It may be that your child would benefit from some additional time with the teacher.

Tutoring

If you try regular extra help sessions with the teacher, and that still doesn't work, you might consider finding a professional tutor to work with your child. In some cases, outside tutoring may be a temporary measure used to help get your child up to speed in an individual course. In other cases, the tutoring relationship may need to be more long term in the event of a persistent weakness within a particular discipline. Tutoring can offer continual reinforcement of concepts and facts that enhances learning and leads to success.

To find a tutor, ask for referrals from your child's teacher, your school's guidance counselor, or friends who may have experienced similar difficulties with their children. Consideration of your child's schedule and commitments, as well as yours, is important as you begin to look for a tutor. Finding an individual who can work with your child at times that are both convenient and effective study times for him is key.

There are individuals, often current teachers, retired educators, or college or graduate students, who work regularly as tutors. As you interview tutors, be sure to ask for and check references. It is important, though, once you feel you have found someone with appropriate credentials, that you choose an individual who will be able to develop a strong rapport with your child. As in any educational relationship, it is important for your child to develop a sense of trust and confidence in the tutor, which will not be possible if he does not engage with the person with whom he is working.

In addition to tutors who work on their own, soliciting their own business, there are professional agencies that offer tutoring services. There are some national chains as well as local or regional businesses working as tutors. In most cases, such agencies will have a center where services can be offered, in addition to sending tutors to the child's home. Depending on your home environment, securing tutoring services at another location may be helpful. If, for instance, you have other children who may be noisy or distracting to the tutoring session, taking your child to an on-site tutoring center may be the best solution.

Fees for tutoring can be substantial. If the fees are prohibitive for your circumstances, you might want to check first with your school personnel, as they may know of community resources that are free or significantly less expensive than tutoring agencies or individuals working for themselves. If your school does not have information, check with libraries, local colleges and universities, community centers, and even high schools that may have students who offer tutoring services to younger children as part of a community service program.

Coaches

For most of us, the term "coach" probably conjures up images of workout gear-clad, physically fit individuals sporting whistles and giving pep talks. Traditionally, coaches have existed primarily in athletics. Recently, however, coaches have entered the academic and business worlds, working with students and professionals to increase productivity and effectiveness. Without actually completing tasks for the student, a coach guides him in determining what he wants to accomplish and the steps needed to get there. Coaches can be particularly helpful to students who have difficulty getting and staying organized or who are inconsistent in their efforts. Coaches help students remain focused and moving toward their goals. The services of a coach may not be for every student but if you have a child who is struggling with the mechanics of organization or is erratic in his effort, a coach may be something to consider.

Middle School—What Is It For?

As your child enters and proceeds through middle school, it is important to remember just what these years are for. These middle years will form the foundation for academic success in high school, which, in turn, brings success in college and beyond. The middle school years should be a time of getting rid of any weaknesses if they exist and preparing for the increased demands and autonomy of high school.

As important as building an academic foundation during the middle school years, however, is creating a strong emotional base. The middle school years bring the beginning of adolescence and the turbulence that can sometimes accompany it. As a child moves into high school and the associated independence it affords and requires, it is essential that he have a strong sense of himself and his values. High school is a time when students are required to take more responsibility for themselves in the classroom and out. A child who is confident in himself and his ability to make choices is more likely to make his own decisions, hopefully good ones, as opposed to going along with the crowd. A child who brings strong study skills, a solid academic foundation, and confidence to his first year of high school will be more likely to find academic and social success, making for a more productive and successful high school career overall.

QUESTIONS TO ASK

- How is my child doing academically?
- What are the child's teacher's expectations or recommendations for duration and type of study and homework sessions each night?
- Are there weaknesses in his background that require tutoring or additional work of any kind?
- Given my child's classroom performance and his homework, quiz, test and project grades, does he seem to be employing effective study skills?
- What are your recommendations for test preparation?
- Is my child exhibiting any particular weaknesses and, if so, what do you recommend we do to address them?

A CHECKLIST FOR SUCCESSFUL STUDY SKILLS IN MIDDLE SCHOOL

- ❑ Be sure your child has an organized, well-lit work space in an area without undue distraction for homework and studying.
- ❑ Be sure your child has the proper school supplies for each class and that suit his own strengths and weaknesses and organizational style.
- ❑ Help your child develop a daily schedule that incorporates school, personal responsibilities, chores, homework, and activities.

❑ Work with your child to manage long-term projects, mapping out a plan to complete small components of it over a reasonable period of time.

❑ If your child is not succeeding academically, confer with his teacher and determine if a tutor is necessary.

❑ If tutoring is necessary, utilize the resources available to you to find an appropriate and effective match for your child.

❑ Help your child with homework and projects but do not complete them for him.

❑ Help your child prepare for tests and quizzes by developing questions about the relevant material and working together on the exercises to be sure he knows it.

Chapter 4
College Admissions
Myth vs. Reality

As the process of applying to college has become more complex and competitive, the mystique surrounding it has grown. At the nation's most competitive colleges, where the acceptance rate has dropped well below 20 percent, in some cases as low as 11 percent, it is often difficult to understand just how admissions decisions are made. It is easy to describe the process as a "crap shoot" when viewing it from the outside; it is simply difficult to understand what makes one straight-A student with outstanding standardized test scores more appealing than another. Additionally, the anecdotal information that is passed along within a school or community adds to the lack of understanding about the process. Everyone knows someone who had all As, was president of this club and head of that activity, had "great" SAT scores, and still didn't get into the college of her choice. Conversely, everyone has also heard of the weak student who had poor test scores who got into a top school. The rumors then fly that it was because her dad "knew" someone or she won an athletic scholarship. In most cases, neither is probably true. It is important to point out that rarely has anyone actually seen the academic credentials of another student. The perception is that the student is a strong or weak applicant when in fact, the reality may be different. It is important to remember that unless you've seen the transcript and score reports, you shouldn't draw conclusions. For example, the straight-A student may have all As in a weak course of study. Such a transcript is not the record that will provide access to top colleges and the rumored "great" SAT scores may not be a reality. The weak student with "poor" test scores may have a very rigorous course load and do well in it, which could offset lower test scores, if they exist, in the eyes of an admissions officer. The point is, until you have sat behind the desk of an admissions officer, it is impossible to understand the breadth and depth of the applicant pool. There are many stories surrounding college admissions that are legendary and should be viewed as that—merely myth not fact.

As parents, we are particularly susceptible to these myths. We want to believe that merely knowing someone at a particular college will help our children gain admission, that a weak student can get into a great school, or that when a great student is denied admission, it is the result of a flawed system. All of these circumstances allow us to believe that we can control the process or provide an excuse when our child isn't accepted. Feeling in control is something we yearn for as parents. Unfortunately, it probably isn't a feeling we experience often, beginning when our toddler threw herself to the floor in a full-blown tantrum or when our five-year-old headed off to kindergarten. As parents, we entrust our children to the educational system and when we do, we give up control of a huge portion of their lives. This step is monumental for us and them, and as our children enter middle school and approach high school, the stakes rise, as does our fear. As a result we seek to control the situation in any way we can. The notion that the college admissions process can be controlled, however, is erroneous. As parents, it is our job to understand what we can influence and what we can't. It is important, therefore, for parents to understand what truly impacts an admissions decision and what does not.

Qualified vs. Competitive

One of the most difficult concepts of the college admissions process to grasp is the idea that a student may be qualified for admission but not competitive. Most students who complete a rigorous college preparatory high school course of study and who have strong standardized test scores are qualified for admission to even the most prestigious colleges. The term "qualified" means that a student is academically and intellectually capable of completing the college or university's curriculum successfully. The student has the skills needed to meet the college's minimum graduation requirements. "Competitive," however, refers to the student's relative strength in the school's applicant pool. A competitive student not only possesses the skills needed to graduate, she exceeds them. Additionally, she is more appealing than other applicants. How appealing a student is can often be influenced by the acceptance rate of the college. As the acceptance rate rises, the level of relative appeal needed for admission declines. At the nation's most competitive colleges, it is likely that 75–80 percent of the applicants for admission are qualified to handle the school's workload. Unfortunately, at schools that accept only 20 percent of the students who apply, 55–60 percent of the qualified applicants are denied. It is important, therefore, to consider not only the average credentials of the school's admitted students, but the acceptance rate as well. Because of the uncertainty inherent in the college admissions processes at schools with such low acceptance rates, students and parents should be cautious about considering only these types of schools when the time to be looking for colleges arrives. While it may be somewhat easy to figure out how many students your child needs to be more appealing than in order to gain admission, it is quite difficult to determine what characteristics will make your child one of those attractive enough to be selected. Understandably, it is this question that seems to spawn the most misunderstanding. Below are some common misperceptions to avoid.

Quotas

One myth that persists in admissions is that there is a quota system in place that limits the number of students from any one high school or region that can be admitted each year. At the nation's most prestigious colleges, those with the lowest acceptance rates, it is easy to believe there is a limit on the number of students from one school that can be admitted. It seems that only one or two, if that, are accepted each year. The reality, though, is that at such schools the mathematics of admissions dictate that a very small percentage of students be admitted; the likelihood that several from one school would be is slim.

The idea of racial quotas is controversial as well and the topic of affirmative action never ceases to spawn debate. In the summer of 2003, the United States Supreme Court issued an endorsement of the use of affirmative action programs in college admissions by upholding the admissions practices of the University of Michigan Law School by a 5–4 vote. Despite a 6–3 vote of the Court, which found the undergraduate admissions practices at the university unconstitutional, supporters of affirmative action view the Court's decisions as a victory overall for such programs. Although on the surface the split decision, with one very close judgment in favor of affirmative action and a more lopsided decision seemingly opposed to it, does not seem likely to be categorized as a victory, together, the decisions can be viewed as a cumulative success. The close 5–4 vote supports Michigan's law school admissions process and confirms the idea that the basis for affirmative action is sound. While the 6–3 vote invalidates the standardized approach used by the undergraduate admissions program at Michigan to enhance the likelihood of acceptance for students of color, the finding in favor of the law school's program allows the existence of efforts to increase minority enrollment through affirmative action. Herein lies the notion of success for supporters.

There are few issues that inspire the strong and often polarized opinions of affirmative action. Whatever your thoughts on the subject, it is important to understand how these Court judgments affect the field of college admissions in general. As with many U.S. institutions, American colleges and universities value diverse constituencies. Most American colleges believe that a diverse student body positively impacts the educational experience of all its students, both in the classroom and out. It is important for students to understand different perspectives and to learn how to interact successfully with people whose background and experiences are different from their own. For this reason, colleges and universities seek to enroll international students as well as American students of color. Interactions between students from different racial and cultural backgrounds allow all those who participate to gain the valuable interpersonal skills needed to achieve success in our increasingly diverse and global society and economy.

While admissions offices develop strategic recruitment efforts to attract students of color, and student affairs divisions implement aggressive retention programs, the number of students involved is often quite small. This point is key to understanding how the Supreme Court's judgment will continue to affect college admissions decisions. First of all, not all students of color admitted to college are beneficiaries of affirmative action programs. To believe this is to discount the accomplishments of many talented young men and women. Also, the percentage of students who are admitted to colleges and universities under affirmative action programs is very small. At least as many students, if not more, are admitted through university efforts to admit strong athletic prospects, children of alumni, and students whose families represent attractive development possibilities. Finally, students admitted under an affirmative action program are qualified students. Accommodations may be made that allow them to be competitive when they otherwise might not be, but all are qualified for admission and are capable of satisfying the college's graduation requirements. The 2003 Supreme Court decisions, therefore, should be viewed not as a program that limits access to college admission for majority students but as a victory for all students, as it will allow colleges and universities to continue to create diverse communities of learning.

The "Hook"

In today's society, who one knows can have a tremendous impact on one's success. It is logical, therefore, to assume that the same is true in the case of the college application process. While it is true that there are admissions cases each year, even at the most competitive schools in the country, that are decided in the student's favor because she is the child or grandchild of a wealthy, prominent, or influential alumnus, there are at least as many cases, and most likely more, that are not successful. It is also important to know that colleges typically only give an advantage to the child of a major supporter, not the niece, nephew, or family friend of said benefactor. In something of a networking mentality, as when beginning a job search, families think they can search their memory bank or Rolodex for the name of the person they met on a plane who knows someone at a particular college. Such casual acquaintances, and even those more substantial, most likely won't have a significant impact on an admissions decision. Truth be told, even if the connected individual has significant "pull" to influence an admissions decision, they most likely will do so only for the people closest to them. And, they won't do it so often as to not dilute the impact of their influence. Additionally, what it takes to be an alumnus who is influential enough to actually change an admissions decision varies from school to school and is conversely proportionate to the level of competition present in the school's application process. In other words, if the school's acceptance rate is 10 percent, the level of involvement required to be influential might be a building bearing the family name. At less competitive schools, merely consistent support for the school, either through active participation in programs or through regular annual giving, may suffice. Relying, therefore, upon an alumni tie or other personal connection for admission is not wise, and it is imperative that when the time comes to apply to college, you and your child include mostly schools for which she is competitive for admission based upon her own merits.

The Jock

We see them on Saturday afternoons and during "March Madness," the athletic elite who represent universities from the ACC to the Ivy League. Regardless of our view of organized sports and their place in higher education, we each have some set of beliefs about the role of athletic prowess in the admissions process. For some, we assume that the starters on the football or basketball team gained admission to their college solely for the contributions they had the potential to make on the athletic field or court. Others, though, may look at star athletes and see the path to college access their own child might take. No matter what your perspective, it is important to understand just how few students gain admission to college as a result of their athletic skills or potential. Additionally, while some (and it's important to note that *some*, not all) athletes receive preferential treatment in the admissions process, student-athletes gain admission to colleges where they might not normally be considered competitive applicants, students who seem unqualified to meet the school's graduation requirements are rarely admitted.

For those parents who see athletics as the ticket to college for their child, it is important to understand just how rare admission based on athletic talent is. According to the National Collegiate Athletic Association's (NCAA) web site, 355,688 students played varsity sports at the nation's colleges and universities during the 2000–2001 school year. That same year, approximately 15,300,000 students were enrolled in four-year colleges and universities (Department of Education web site). In other words, only 2.3 percent of all college students were student athletes. Because these numbers tend to remain fairly similar from year to year, it's fair to assume that the rate of participation in 2001–2002 is a good indicator of prior and future years. Because not all of those participating in college athletics were recruited as part of their admission process, it is safe to conclude that even fewer than 2.3 percent of all admissions decisions were based on athletic talent. Even those who receive significant attention from college coaches during initial stages of the college search process may not ultimately be an admissions priority for the coach and, as a result, may not be admitted. Seeking to fully cover real or potential holes in athletic squads, coaches woo many high school athletes over the course of several months as they try to find students who will meet their needs and admissions requirements. While coaches will provide admissions directors with priority lists of athletic recruits, the final admissions decision rests solely in the admissions office.

If yours is the child who has made the "select" or "travel" team each time the opportunity was available, or the one who has physical attributes and the strong gross motor skills that enhance athletic abilities, you may have a child who might eventually be capable of considering college athletics. If you have such a child, you probably wonder how, or maybe if, you should maximize it. You might wonder if you should help your child pursue college athletics because you recognize the high pressure of such an involvement. Or, it might be that you doubt whether such an all-consuming focus is healthy and appropriate for your child. If you want to help your child to pursue this avenue, your child's coaches and instructors can help you determine if, in fact, the child has the innate skills and potential to become a high-caliber athlete. As they become available and age-appropriate, registering your child for sports showcases and camps that are observed by college, and even high school, coaches may be something to consider. Beware, though, that if coaches find your child an appealing athlete, they will begin to contact your family and to pursue your child with fervor and persistence. Such attention, while flattering, can bring significant pressure that may be difficult to manage. Therefore, families should enter the ring of college admissions as a prospective athletic recruit with care and forethought.

The Only Weaknesses Are Her Grades and Test Scores

Some families begin the college search process thinking that it is the extra qualities their child possesses that will allow her to gain admission to college. When describing their child's characteristics, parents speak proudly of the student government offices held, the volunteer work completed, and the unique activities participated in. They close the description with the disclaimer, sometimes quite cavalierly, "it's only her test scores and grades that are a little weak." The fact is that unless your child is uniquely talented, achieving recognition at a regional, state, or national level, her test scores and grades are paramount to the admissions decision-making process and must not be dismissed as a trivial or a secondary consideration. The threshold that these academic credentials must exceed is even higher the more competitive admission to the school is.

Choosing Extracurricular Activities

Some parents seek to find the "right" extracurricular activity on which their child should focus. What is important to remember is that one can never predict who will be on the receiving end of an application. And, activities (and the time devoted to them) chosen for some sort of perceived value in the admissions process as opposed to the most important criteria, their appeal to the child, could be meaningless if she isn't admitted to the selected college of choice. You can avoid this potential result if the child has a say in choosing activities and makes the decision about her commitments without regard to its influence on the college search. The child also begins to learn about making good and thoughtful decisions in a safe and forgiving setting and period in her life. As in the academic realm, the middle school years are a great testing ground for activities and personal pursuits. Certainly, learning the importance of making and keeping a commitment is important, but experimenting with different interests in order to find those most enjoyable during this time is valuable as well.

The danger in trying to handpick activities based upon how they might influence the future is that as individuals we all have prejudices and things we find appealing. As a result, trying to select just the right activity for a young child to present as a strength at the time of her college application years later is not rational. As mentioned earlier, children should be encouraged to find their particular interests and to develop those interests to a level that is comfortable and appropriate for them. In recent years there have been a number of articles and papers written by individuals either actively involved in the college admissions process or closely related. In an attempt to position children well, parents sometimes adopt a "more is better" approach. It is essential to remember that, as in many facets of life, quality, not quantity, is what is important.

The Harvard Admissions Staff narrative, "Time Out or Burn Out for the Next Generation," focuses on the increasing pressure placed on today's children to be successful and the often well-meaning but ill-conceived path to this achievement. The article highlights the extreme efforts many families will go to in order to position their children for successful admission to college. The outcome can be students who are not able to discover, let alone pursue, activities that are of genuine interest to them. They argue that children forced to follow a specific path either stumble along the way as they realize they are not being true to themselves or find themselves as unfulfilled adults who have followed a path to success that appears satisfying but is not because it is based on the goals and desire of others—even if those others are the people who know them best, their parents. The looming thought of college and gaining admission to the right school is the driving force behind the pressure families feel to enroll children in a multitude of extracurricular and academic enrichment activities.

While competition to the nation's most prestigious colleges is keen, and there is no formula to predict who will be admitted, the message seems clear. Colleges and universities want to see applicants who have achieved balance in their lives and have pursued activities of genuine interest to them. Parents should afford children the opportunity to discover and cultivate their own passions. Such an approach will allow the child to develop into a fulfilled individual, a goal that is valuable regardless of where she eventually enrolls for college.

Managing the Stress of Today's Lifestyles

In its article, the Harvard admission staff promotes two ideas for families to help manage the stress of today's active lifestyles:

- Families should allow for "downtime" and should spend it together. As parents' jobs and children's schedules become more demanding, spending time together becomes more difficult and at the same time more needed.
- Harvard also advises families to "bring back summer." No one suggests that summer should be a time for TV watching and other sedentary activities, but it should be a time for students to reflect and refocus and experience a change of pace from the school year.

As Harvard's article concludes: "Parents and students alike could profit from redefining success as fulfillment of the students' own aims, usually yet to be discovered." The result will be a young adult with unique passions and interests. The genuine commitment your child makes to activities she has selected and the passion with which she can express the impact of her experiences to others will be much more influential to her future college choices than a laundry list of "right" activities that have no intrinsic value to the student. And, hopefully, children and parents can have more time and more enjoyable experiences together.

Understanding the Role of Admissions Officers

The field of college admissions attracts individuals who possess a number of common personality traits. In general, admissions officers, especially those who tend to conduct the most admissions interviews and who visit high schools, are approachable, friendly, and enthusiastic. At best, the enthusiasm and interest in students is genuine and the admissions officer entered the field because he truly wants to help students and families find a good college match. At worst, the admissions officer, concerned with meeting the recruitment expectations of his job, may be overly encouraging simply to meet dictated goals. The point here for parents is that you need to help your child understand the public relations efforts of colleges. Everyone must recognize that, while in very few cases an admission decision for an applicant may be shifted in the student's favor because of a very positive interview or meeting with an individual admissions officer, generally a friendly, encouraging admissions professional is just doing his job. And, while the admissions officer may indeed really like your child, that alone will not make her qualified or competitive for admission.

Important Factors in Admissions Decisions

After you realize what *won't* influence your child's chances for admission, you will wonder what *will* and in what proportion.

High School Record

Without doubt, the single most important factor an admissions officer considers when determining whether or not to admit a student is the high school record. The high school record, as discussed earlier, is the full complement of courses taken, how well the student has done in them, and where such courses place the student within the context of her school. For example, if your child enrolls in all honors level courses and does very well but does not take any of the Advanced Placement courses available to her at the high school, then she could be viewed as not being willing to pursue challenges. While college admissions officers don't want students to overextend themselves, they do find students who take appropriate academic risks appealing. After all, without risk, students can't reach their full potential.

Other Factors

As included in the earlier discussion of the basics of college admission, a variety of factors influence an admission decision in addition to the student's high school record. Standardized test scores, extracurricular activities, teacher recommendations, and an essay or personal statement all come into play when determining whether or not a student will gain admission to a college. It is important to remember that no one factor solely determines admission. Academic credentials, the high school record in particular, carry more weight than nonacademic ones, but it is the trends and overall image created by the student's credentials upon which admissions officers make their decisions.

When a student possesses a particularly strong profile in a single area, it is easy to believe that credentials alone will sway an admissions decision. If the area of strength is the student's grades, it is understandable why parents might believe the admissions decision will be based on it. Each year, however, there are class valedictorians who are not admitted to their first choice college. Sometimes this is the case because the colleges to which they apply are so competitive that admissions staff members are choosing between too many equally strong candidates. Sometimes, though, it is because there is a weakness in the student's record that isn't readily apparent by a review of her GPA or class standing. If the student has not taken a solid college preparatory course load, strong performance in classes that will not be good preparation for college is irrelevant.

Standardized Test Scores

If a parent wants to place a bet on one application component carrying more weight in the selection process, his money is best wagered on the academic record rather than test scores (see the following chapter). High standardized test scores, though, seem to instill a false sense of security when it comes to college admission. After all, good performance on either the SAT I or the ACT is easy to understand and conceptualize. The score report sent to families includes information about where the student stands relative to all the other students across the country who took the same test. If the student compares most favorably, it is easy to believe that scores alone will bring the student admission success. Because admissions officers look for trends within the application, however, if the test scores present a very different picture of the student relative to her high school record, they can actually harm her chances for admission.

Generally, if the student's test scores are weak relative to her grades, the perception is that the student may be achieving more than she should. Such a circumstance is a positive from an admissions perspective. If the test scores are high enough to warrant admission, and if the competition of the school's admissions process is reasonable enough to allow a student with somewhat weaker scores, such a student may be admitted ahead of other students with stronger standardized test performance. A student, however, whose grades are low relative to her standardized test scores and without other extenuating circumstances, such as personal health issues or socioeconomic factors, which may impede performance, risks being viewed as an underachiever. Such a perception is very unappealing in the admissions process as colleges, like most institutions, want to welcome into their communities individuals who make the most of their opportunities and skills. In short, they don't have evidence that the student will perform as well as possible and may not be willing to give such a student a place in their class.

The definition and response to an "underachiever," however, will vary from college to college. A particularly competitive college may simply not have room to take a student who exhibits exceptional innate intellectual ability as a result of test scores because there are other students who will have similar testing but better classroom performance who will also be denied admission. A college whose admissions program is somewhat less competitive, however, may have more flexibility in admission and might be willing to give such a student a chance for the sake of their potential. Parents need to remember, though, that admissions decisions are rarely made solely on the basis of potential but rather a combination of potential and achievement.

The Bottom Line

There are likely many areas in which you, as a parent, feel responsible for the success or failure of your child. In some areas, parents are responsible—we must provide a safe and secure home environment for our children, we need to be engaged in their lives outside the family to ensure their safety, and we need to be certain they have the resources they need to be successful in school. The college admissions process, though, is different. Throughout the complicated process of getting into college, it is essential that students and parents remember that self-worth, as a parent or a child, should not be tied to where a student applies or is admitted to college. If the parents have provided the best educational opportunities to which they have access, along with the support and guidance needed to help the student to be motivated for academic success, and if the child has done her best, then everyone has met their responsibility and should feel good about the experience and any achievements. It is the accomplishment of meeting these goals, not the receipt of a particular college acceptance letter, that merits value as a measure of one's self-worth.

- What does my child like to do and what is she good at?
- Is my child exceptionally talented in a specific area?
- What kind of extracurricular and cultural opportunities are available through my child's school and community?
- Am I pushing my child too hard?
- Does my child have a healthy balance of academic and personal activities?
- Is my child able to make a commitment?

A Checklist for Making Decisions Based on Facts Not Myths

❑ Be realistic in understanding and perception of your child's strengths and weaknesses.

❑ Seek "expert" evaluation and guidance when your child appears to exhibit extraordinary talents and skills.

❑ Provide opportunities for your child to test her areas of interest and be exposed to things unfamiliar to her.

Chapter 5

Standardized Testing
A Primer

Whether it is because they took it as part of their own college application process or because of the ubiquitous articles about it, its influence, and its evolution, even the parents of young children are aware of the SAT, the best-known of standardized tests. The SAT, developed by the Educational Testing Service and first administered by the College Entrance Examination Board (now commonly known as the College Board) in 1926 (College Board web site, 2003), has become a driving force in college admissions and has become influential outside academia as well. An entire industry dedicated to preparing students for the SAT has emerged and there are a number of multimillion-dollar corporations as well as many local businesses offering such services. A test designed for one very specific purpose has become an American icon with impact beyond its natural sphere of influence and, therefore, is quite intriguing; that is, if you've already gone to college and don't have the three-hour, Saturday morning exam in your future!

In 1926 college-bound students had only one test to take, the SAT. The original SAT has evolved over the years and is the predecessor of today's SAT I. While the SAT is still the dominant test in the college application process, today's students have other options available to them. The College Board sponsors the PSAT, the Preliminary Scholastic Assessment Test, which serves as practice for college- and, therefore, SAT-bound students. It also offers discipline-based tests called SAT IIs or "Subject Tests," which allow students to illustrate particular strength in specific academic areas. The SAT IIs are the current version of the Achievement Tests that some parents may have taken as part of their own college search. Some colleges and universities will require both the SAT I and SAT II for admission. The scoring scale for both exams is 200 to 800.

In the late 1950s the American College Testing Program was founded and the ACT was introduced. While this test was once rather limited in its use and exposure, today students across the country take the exam each year and some choose to submit only their ACT results as part of their college application process. There is a practice version of the ACT available as well that is called the PLAN and is typically available to sophomores in schools that utilize it. The scoring for the PLAN is a 1 to 32 scale, while the ACT is scored on a 1 to 36 scale.

SAT I
A History of America's Most Influential Test

When the College Board first offered the SAT in 1926, just over 8,000 students took the exam (College Board web site, 2003). Those who took the test were white males from the higher economic levels of American society. According to College Board data, during the 2001–2002 school year, more than 2 million students took the SAT; more of the test takers were female than male with a 54:46 female:male ratio, and 35 percent were students of color, the highest proportion to date (College Board web site, 2003). Because college is no longer accessible to just those of significant financial means, the SAT is no longer taken by only those in the upper classes.

As a result, over the course of its history, the test itself has evolved in response to the changes in the population of test takers. From its inception, the SAT has included items to test students' verbal and math skills. Verbal test sections have included antonyms, analogies, and reading comprehension items, while the math sections have covered the concepts of algebra I and geometry. While there have been some changes in the content and format of the SAT over the years, none have compared to the complete overhaul of the exam that began in 2002. The new SAT I, to be administered for the first time in March 2005, will be significantly different from the previous version in both format and content.

The new exam will include three sections: critical reading (replacing the former "verbal section"), math, and writing. The 200 to 800 score scale will remain the same but the perfect combined score will increase from 1600 to 2400 to reflect the addition of the third section. The critical reading portion will include sections requiring students to identify sentence errors, improve sentences, and improve paragraphs. The math section will include concepts from algebra II in addition to algebra I and geometry. For more specific information about the structure and concepts included in the new SAT I, parents and students can visit the College Board's web site and select the menu for the New SAT.

Trends in SAT I Scores

Over the past 30 years, the racial and gender composition of the test-taking population has changed significantly and the average SAT I scores have fluctuated somewhat. There has been some improvement in math scores but a significant decline in the verbal section has occurred. In addition to changes in content and format, the scoring of the SAT has been altered as well. In 1995 the SAT scales were replaced because the average scores had fallen below the "expected" score of 500 on each section. This change is known as "recentering," and while there was some initial shifting in scores, the notion of what a specific score means has once again settled and test takers have a firm understanding of their results.

A review of recentered scores from 1972 to 2002 shows that the average verbal score dropped from 530 in 1972 to 504 in 2002, while the average math score improved from 509 in 1972 to 516 in 2002. These statistics represent the average score, which includes the results of all, both male and female, test takers. When reviewing scores by gender, young men still score higher on both portions of the SAT I although the gap is narrowing. The document, "10-Year Trend in SAT Scores Indicates Increased Emphasis on Math Is Yielding Results; Reading and Writing Are Causes for Concern," issued by the College Board in August 2002, asserts that the national effort to improve math education in the United States has been successful and has led to the highest average math score in 32 years. While the math score in 2002 is a full 15 points higher than the median 10 years earlier, the average verbal score is only 4 points higher.

The College Board points to increased enrollment in higher-level math courses as the reason for improvement. "Forty-five percent of this year's college-bound seniors took precalculus in high school, up from 33 percent just a decade ago. Participation in calculus also increased over the past decade from 20 percent in 1992 to 25 percent." The trends in academic preparation and the associated score increase suggest it is in the best interest of students to pursue the most rigorous course of study appropriate to their abilities and interests. It is important that parents understand the abilities and goals of their children and play an active role in school course selection throughout the middle and high school years in order to ensure that they have access to the types of courses that will prepare them for success in the classroom and on standardized tests.

Students with Learning Differences and Other Special Needs

For years the College Board and ACT have allowed accommodations to the testing environment and even the test format for students with documented learning differences and/or physical disabilities. Students with attention deficit disorder (ADD) are able to take the exams in quiet, less distracting settings. Students with visual deficits can request large-print exams. The most common accommodation, however, is the allowance of extended time. It is most important for parents of children who will need accommodations to remember to be in close contact with the Services for Students with Disabilities (SSD) Coordinator at your child's school in order to be sure you meet all requirements and deadlines necessary to receive needed allowances.

In order to receive testing accommodations on exams administered by the College Board and ACT, students must be able to document the need for such allowances. This documentation must take the form of a psychoeducational evaluation from a licensed professional for those requesting accommodations for learning differences. Documentation from a medical professional is required for those students requesting accommodations for physical challenges. Currently, the documentation provided must be from an evaluation completed within the three years prior to the proposed test date.

For years, the standardized test scores of students who received any type of accommodations were "flagged" by an asterisk on the score report, indicating to those who evaluated the scores that the administration was nonstandard. After a number of years of lobbying and debate, the College Board has agreed to eliminate the flagging of scores obtained through a nonstandard test administration beginning with tests given in October 2003. Score reports sent after October 1, 2003, for any test date will not include flags either. This decision is viewed as a significant victory as there can no longer be the perception that there is any stigma attached to or discounting of scores obtained in a nonstandard setting. It is important for the parents of students who will require testing accommodations to recognize that these allowances are in place for students who truly warrant them. In order to allow your child to exhibit his potential it is necessary to seek and utilize the appropriate adjustments to test site, time allotment, or test format.

The Actual Tests

For the uninitiated, navigating the waters of the standardized testing required of the college-bound student can be a daunting task. Fortunately, there is significant information available to help parents and students prepare for this hurdle in the college application process. The College Board and ACT web sites offer a tremendous amount of information regarding their respective exams along with preparation suggestions and exercises such as "the SAT word of the day." Periodic visits to these web sites will allow parents to stay abreast of any changes to the tests and to become aware of what the actual test makers recommend for test preparation as the test date for their children approaches.

PSAT: The Preliminary Scholastic Assessment Test

Designed as a practice test for the Scholastic Assessment Test, or SAT I, the PSAT is an abbreviated version of it that provides students with exposure to the various types of questions and the test format they will encounter when they take the SAT I. While many high schools administer the PSAT to sophomores to provide additional exposure to the exam, the test itself is designed for juniors. Only juniors are eligible for the National Merit Scholarship Competition for which the PSAT is the qualifying exam. There are three sections on the PSAT including verbal, math, and writing. The individual sections of the PSAT are scored on a scale from 20 to 80. The planned changes to the SAT I will influence the PSAT and a new format will be introduced for the October 2004 exam.

PLAN: A Practice ACT

The PLAN is an exam administered by the American College Testing Program and serves as a practice instrument for the ACT. The PLAN is designed for sophomores and is a more curriculum-based exam than either the PSAT or SAT I. As is the case with the ACT, there are four subsections of the PLAN including English, science reasoning, math, and reading. The four subscores are used to calculate a composite. The highest score possible on the PLAN is 32.

SAT I: Scholastic Assessment Test

The SAT I is the standardized test most often required for admission to American colleges and universities. The SAT I, as noted above, will undergo a complete revision of its format and the new test will be administered for the first time in the spring of 2005. The new test will include three sections: critical reading, writing, and math. Each individual section will be scored on a 200 to 800 scale with 2400 as the highest possible score.

SAT II: Subject Tests

In addition to the SAT I, the College Board also administers the SAT II Subject Tests. Offered in 22 fields, the SAT IIs allow students to demonstrate in-depth knowledge in a variety of arenas. While not universally required for admission purposes, many colleges and universities do recommend that students take at least three SAT II exams, currently including the Writing Subject Test, and will use these test scores when determining an admissions decision. The SAT II results can also be required for placement purposes upon matriculation at the student's college of choice. Students must be sure to research the test requirements of the individual colleges in which they are interested to insure that any required SAT IIs are completed.

For a relatively brief period, the College Board allowed students to elect to participate in the "Score Choice" program when taking the SAT II. Score Choice allowed students to see their SAT II scores before deciding whether or not they could be viewed by colleges. If a student's scores were held under Score Choice, they would not be included on the cumulative SAT I and II report mailed to colleges. When Score Choice ended in summer 2002, however, students lost the option to hold scores from review by admissions officers and now all SAT score reports include the results of any SAT I and II tests up to that date. Families, therefore, must take care and consult with guidance personnel and teachers when registering for SAT IIs in high school.

ACT

The ACT is a curriculum-based standardized test that is accepted broadly by American colleges and universities. Once a test recognized more readily by institutions in the western and midwestern sections of the country, the ACT is now commonly accepted in addition to or in lieu of the SAT I (and sometimes the SAT II as well) by schools throughout the United States. Like its practice test, the PLAN, the ACT is composed of four sections (English, reading, science reasoning, and math); each receive a score of up to 36 and are used to calculate the composite. Because the ACT is curriculum-based, students who complete a rigorous and challenging course of study will often score well on the exam. It is possible for a student to earn a comparatively higher score on the ACT than the SAT I so it is recommended that students sit for at least one administration of the ACT.

Remember, each college or university has its own testing requirements. It is essential to research carefully the admissions guidelines of each school to insure that the testing requirements of each are met. For more information about these standardized tests, visit their web sites. These sites include information about the content, format, and scoring of the tests in addition to practice questions and test preparation hints. For the PSAT, SAT I, and SAT II see *www.collegeboard.com*. For the PLAN and ACT see *www.act.org*.

Sample Testing Sequence

Although high school guidance offices will remind students of registration deadlines and may offer suggestions about when admissions tests should be taken, parents should take an active role in the registration and preparation process. Parents should familiarize themselves with their child's curriculum and determine the best standardized testing sequence. Below is a sample test calendar that may be appropriate.

Sophomore Year

- PSAT—Administered mid-October on a national test date; registration is normally coordinated through the student's school
- PLAN—Administered at the school's discretion and on a date of its choosing

Junior Year

- PSAT—Administered mid-October on a national test date; registration is normally coordinated through the student's school. The junior year PSAT is the qualifying test for the National Merit Scholarship Program.
- SAT I—The test is available throughout the year but taking the SAT I on the January or March/April (the test date changes from year to year) test date is advisable as it allows families to obtain early a key piece of information that will drive the college search.
- ACT—The ACT is available throughout the year but the April test date is a convenient time, late enough in the junior year that students have completed a significant portion of their curriculum, thereby offering strong preparation for a curriculum-based test like the ACT.
- SAT II—The SAT II is available periodically throughout the year but the June test date is advisable as it allows students to prepare concurrently for both the SAT II tests and their courses' final exams. Completing SAT IIs in June is especially important for students who may decide to apply to college under an Early Action or Early Decision program.

Senior Year

- ACT and SAT I/SAT II—There are numerous administrations of all three exams throughout the fall. Students who are not satisfied with the results of their junior year exams should plan to sit for the ACT and/or SAT during the fall. Many, but not all, colleges will accept scores from tests taken through the January test date of the senior year; be sure to check the admissions literature of the schools in which you are interested for testing requirements.

The National Merit Scholarship Program

The National Merit Scholarship Program is a recognition program based upon performance on the PSAT. Although ninth- and tenth-graders can all take the PSAT, if sanctioned by their school, only the scores earned on an administration taken during the junior year qualify students for participation in the National Merit Scholarship Program.

There are a number of levels of recognition in the National Merit Program. The first is "Commended Student" status, which is based solely on the score earned on the PSAT. The three scores from each of the subsections of the PSAT discussed below are combined to determine a student's selection index.

- A student with a selection index of 200 or higher is recognized as a "Commended Student"; about 2.6 percent of the students who take the PSAT achieve this level.
- The next level of recognition in the program is that of National Merit "Semi-Finalist." Because the National Merit Program strives for geographic diversity in its recognition, "the top-scoring" participants in each state are named Semifinalists (National Merit Scholarship Corporation, 2003). "The number named in each state is based on the state's percentage of the national total of high school graduating seniors" (National Merit Scholarship Corporation, 2003); the selection index required to achieve this level, therefore, can vary quite significantly and may exceed 215.
- Recognition as a "Finalist" in the National Merit Program is based upon the academic performance or grades, school recommendation, and personal essay of the student. About 90 percent of the semifinalists reach finalist status. Some finalists are designated as Corporate Scholars or receive funding from the college at which they enroll. Selection for this level of recognition is based upon specific criteria determined by the sponsoring corporation or college.

Ultimately, roughly 1 percent of those who take the PSAT reach the Finalist level. Such distinction is impressive and warrants attention from college admissions officers; attention, however, should not be read as "acceptance." The same is true of any level of recognition in the National

Merit Program. While achieving any level is impressive, it may not be distinctive in the college admissions process, especially at extremely competitive schools.

The National Merit Scholarship Corporation also sponsors recognition programs for students of color. Students of color may be recognized by the National Merit Program in addition to one of these special categories. The National Achievement Program recognizes the achievements of African-American students, while the National Hispanic Recognition Program highlights the accomplishments of Hispanic students. Although the number of students impacted by these programs is smaller than that of the National Merit Program, those who participate are, indeed, impressive.

Is Commercial Test Preparation for Your Child?

Each year a question asked often of high school guidance counselors is whether or not a student should enroll in a commercial test preparation course in anticipation of taking the standardized tests required for college admission. While the answer varies from student to student, there are some standard factors to consider when deciding if commercial test preparation is right for your child. Those factors include the average success rate of test preparation, the type of setting that would be best suited to the student, and the student's past standardized test experience.

The maze of test preparation agencies can be as overwhelming as the college search process itself. It seems that everywhere one turns there is an ad for one test preparation organization or another. Friends, acquaintances, and colleagues question a parent's intentions about commercial test preparation organizations or share their own experiences with standardized testing and preparation. To further cloud the issue, the nation's most visible college rankings are produced by publishers with links to Kaplan and the Princeton Review, the premier test preparation organizations. *Time* and Kaplan have teamed up and *Newsweek* and Princeton Review have joined forces to challenge the venerable *U.S. News and World Report* in the battle over ranking the nation's colleges and universities. The decision, however, to enroll in a test preparation course must be made based upon the individual needs and circumstances of your child.

Types of Commercial Test Prep

There are three primary types of commercial test preparation available to students: group courses, one-on-one tutoring, and online preparation. According to the College Board's web site, short-term programs (about 20 hours) improve scores an average of 10 points on verbal and 15 points on math. Longer-term programs (40 hours) improve scores an average of 15–20 points on verbal and 20–30 points on math. (College Board web site, 2003) Courses that teach math content rather than test-taking tips tend to result in better scores. High school students in general can expect their scores to increase each year about 15–20 points on verbal and 15–20 points on math just naturally as their skills develop. Additionally, although students receive an exact score on their score report, the College Board acknowledges that a 30-point range of score variation is possible. Hence, a score increase of up to 30 points may just reflect this natural fluctuation. Students and parents must weigh the time and cost of test preparation programs against the possibility that score increases may not be significant or outside an expected range when deciding whether or not to enroll in a commercial course.

If a student and his parents have determined that they would like to pursue a commercial test preparation course, there are a number of factors to keep in mind:

1. The courses can be expensive. There are some less expensive online options but generally the family will be making a significant investment to enroll in a commercial course.

2. The courses, individual tutoring, or online programs require a substantial time commitment on the part of the student. In order to make enrolling in such a course worthwhile, it is essential that the student not only have the time required for the test preparation but be committed to it as well. The timing of the preparation is important to consider also. If a family decides to pursue test prep, it should take place just prior to the test administration or as close as possible.

3. The student must consider what format is best suited to his learning style. A student who relies on personal attention in order to succeed academically would most likely gain the most from one-on-one tutoring, while a student who does not need such an individualized approach may choose a group setting. Neither type of preparation is better than another; rather, the student's needs and style make one option a better choice.

The Role of the Parent

Although re-creating an SAT-like setting by quizzing a fifth-grader with sentence completion questions, under a time limit, on a Saturday morning is unreasonable and not likely to be very effective at accomplishing much of anything, parents can take a proactive role in helping their children prepare for the idea of standardized tests. Certainly, vocabulary development and encouraging active reading will help children in school and on tests. Making certain that young children grasp the concepts of basic math before moving on to algebra and beyond will help immensely. Parents can also help children develop a healthy perspective on tests; perhaps encouraging a view of them as a challenge or game against themselves to test their own skills and understanding, not determine their self-worth as a person. No test, the SAT included, measures what kind of person a child is nor does it indicate the level of success he can achieve. What standardized tests do offer is information about certain academic skills and this information will help guide families in planning their child's educational future. Important? Yes. Life-determining? No. Parents and students need to put this test and others into perspective.

A Word of Caution

Be careful not to overprepare or create a situation that will cause your child to develop anxiety over the exams. The best preparation any child can have for college entrance exams and school in general is to devote time and effort to strengthening his reading skills. A child who reads often and actively, looking up words he is not familiar with, will develop a strong vocabulary and solid critical reading skills. The student's course of study in school also contributes greatly to the success he is likely to have on standardized tests. As parents, it is important to actively participate in your child's course selection, aiding him in choosing classes that will challenge and prepare him but not overwhelm him.

One final word regarding standardized testing: It is important that when your child embarks on this facet of the college application process everyone understands that performance on the SAT or ACT is not a reflection of a student's intelligence or likelihood for success. Modest scores do not mean that students are unlikely to achieve their goals or will not have access to professional opportunities. Conversely, high test scores do not ensure success. As in any endeavor, students must make the most of their abilities and commit fully to pursuing each opportunity that comes their way, and *that*, not test scores, will bring success.

QUESTIONS TO ASK

- Can someone knowledgeable in the area of testing review my child's standardized testing record with me and offer insight into it?
- What is the standardized testing sequence advocated by the high school my child will attend?
- Is my child likely to be one who would benefit from commercial test preparation?

- What type of test preparation would best suit my child's learning style and personality?
- Will my child need accommodations on standardized tests as a result of a documented learning disability?

A Checklist for Developing a Standardized Testing Plan

❏ Review your child's standardized testing record from elementary and middle school, noting particular strengths and weaknesses.

❏ Periodically review the College Board and ACT web sites for test format and content changes or updates.

❏ Work with your child to develop active reading skills.

❏ Monitor your child's progress in math to be sure he is developing a strong foundation in the concepts necessary for future success.

❏ Be sure any learning disability documentation and accommodation recommendations are current and in the appropriate format.

Chapter 6

Hobbies, Sports, and Other Talents

Their Role in College Admissions

There are reasons that proverbs and popular sayings are passed along from generation to generation, usually because there is at least some kernel of truth to the statement. Such is the case with the phrase, "all work and no play make John a dull boy." Whether you have a John or a Jane in your life, one of the roles a parent should play is that of talent scout and recreational director. As difficult as it may seem to balance these seemingly trivial roles with those such as physician's assistant, tutor, bodyguard, and nutritionist, it is important to help your child discover and foster her personal interests and talents. In addition to the inherent value in being able to relax and pursue hobbies and pastimes, for children with particular talent there may be rewards in the college admissions process and beyond as well.

Getting Involved

Parents of high school students often mistakenly believe that the quantity of activities a student participates in or the type of endeavor is what is important when it comes time to apply to college. Neither is true. College admissions representatives want to see a commitment to extracurricular interests, not merely a laundry list of activities to which the student has devoted neither significant time nor energy. Helping a child to begin to develop interests in middle school, thereby hopefully gaining an understanding of the satisfaction derived from them may encourage them to take the initiative to get involved once in high school. Admissions officers can easily see through the efforts of a student—whether of her own volition or at her parents' urging—to create an extracurricular résumé in the last two years of high school as the college search process becomes imminent. Beginning to commit to activities and interests in middle school can save both children and parents from this source of anxiety at least.

Extracurricular interests can take many forms. A child's interests may develop as a result of family activities or because of her own strengths and talents. What it is important for parents to remember is that while all activities may not be created equal in the eyes of an admissions officer—facility at the controls of an X-box, for example, is not likely to be as attractive as years of experience playing the saxophone—it is impossible for anyone to predict what will be more appealing when the child applies to college. It is, therefore, pointless to attempt to choose activities for your child based on anything other than her interests or goals.

Too Many Commitments?

In today's American culture, we have reached a point where many of our children are overscheduled and overcommitted. Parents are stressed trying to get their children to each practice, game, rehearsal, and recital, and this anxiety can often be sensed by their kids. In some cases, the child loves what she is doing, but in others the demands of a busy schedule of activities on top of school commitments can be overwhelming and unwanted. Many books and articles have appeared recently that warn against the dangers of children with too many commitments and the negative impact on the structure of today's families. Parents should be reassured that college admissions officers are not looking for quantity with regard to activities on a college application. This reassurance should inspire reason within families when determining what type of activities and how many to devote their cumulative time and effort to.

While all parents act out of concern for their children and a desire to help them reach their full potential, some can make irrational decisions. Often, the motivation behind such choices may be the belief that their child has the opportunity to achieve national recognition or beyond in a chosen activity. The fact of the matter, though, is that very few children have the talent, drive, and focus to achieve at such an elite level, but there are some kids who do. What all parents must remember is that they must keep their child's best interest at heart and use their health and well-being as a barometer for good decision making.

The Tuba or Baseball—What Should You Choose?

For younger children, parents are usually the force behind the decisions about how to spend resources and time. A parent who grew up playing soccer or collecting coins will likely try to pass those same interests along to his child. For parents who did not have the opportunity to engage in organized activities themselves, there may be an urge to push their children into multiple activities indiscriminately in order to make up for some deficiency in their own childhood. While young children may not be able to articulate their preferences, or may be unaware of the options open to them, as they grow they will gain perspective and be able to express their own interests. As their personalities take shape and children begin to make their preferences known, it is important for parents to listen and incorporate them into their own decision-making process.

Because middle schoolers are of an age at which they can express themselves and are beginning to understand themselves on some level, this time period is a great point at which to begin exploring interests on a broader scale. This time frame is a great opportunity to test interests and should be exploited. Schools may offer after-school clubs and sports; community centers may offer classes and leagues; and, students may begin to take the initiative and start their own groups. Whatever avenue is well suited for your child, you should support her involvement in a variety of activities. Showing support for a child's interest, even as she may be showing signs of frustration with you and a desire to distance herself as she begins to define herself, will remind her of your support and concern for her.

The point of pursuing a variety of interests may be simply to help your child find a pastime that she may choose to pursue for years to come. It may also be to help a child find a passion or a significant talent she may possess. As a child enters middle school, natural talents may begin to emerge. In the case of athletics or performing arts, such as dance or vocal music, a child's physical attributes play a critical role in determining the level of talent a child possesses. Because a middle schooler's body is not yet fully developed, particular strength may not be evident or may be exaggerated, only to alter significantly as the child's body continues to mature. Whatever your child's interests or abilities, the middle school years provide a wonderful testing ground for those at which she may excel or choose to continue into high school and beyond.

Extracurricular Activities and the College Admissions Process

Any parent with an eye toward college planning will realize that a student's activities outside of class can play an important role in the college search and application process. For those students with exceptional talent in a particular area, the activity may dictate which colleges they will consider and which schools they will have access to. Students who have made valuable contributions to their schools and communities, but do not possess extraordinary skill in any one area, may not define their college search by activities but will find that the commitment and dedication they have exhibited is appealing to those making the admissions decision on their applications.

How Are Extracurricular Activities Used by Admissions Officers?

Just as there are thousands of colleges and universities across the country, there are thousands of different application forms and application review processes. Some colleges ask simply for biographical and academic information on their application forms. Others not only ask for this information but require an overview of extracurricular involvement, multiple essays requiring significant personal reflection, and personal references that comment on character and academic preparation. Obviously, colleges that don't ask for a listing of activities as part of their application can't routinely consider such involvement when making admissions decisions. Colleges, however, that require this information on their applications are sincerely interested in what a student has done to contribute to her community prior to college, hoping to discern what she may add to their own. Many admissions officers view creating a class, adding to the legacy of the institution through the process of selecting candidates for admission, as an exciting and primary focus of their job. To fulfill this professional responsibility, admissions officers need to understand what motivates and excites an applicant. There are few better ways to do this than by examining what they have devoted their time to and used to channel their passions.

Controlling the Extracurricular Profile

Like the application essay, a student's extracurricular profile is one of the few things she has control over in the admissions process. Unlike the essay, however, an extracurricular résumé can't be developed in an hour, a week, or even a semester. It is up to parents to encourage their children to get involved and pursue their interests at the beginning of high school so they can develop a meaningful roster of extracurricular activities. Although what a student does outside of class can be an important and interesting component of the college application, unless the student possesses significant talent, allowing her to achieve an elite level of performance and recognition, it is unlikely that any extracurricular activity will have the power to change an admissions decision.

Talents and Achievements

Even particular talents or achievements at an elite level, however, will not bring admission to a college for which the student is not prepared or able to succeed in. In such cases, however, students must most likely be "qualified" for admission not "competitive" in an academic sense. It is in no one's best interest—student or college—for a student who is not adequately prepared or intellectually able enough to meet the requirements for graduation. While nonacademic talent will not bring an acceptance to a school the student isn't ready for, it may sway a decision in her favor if she has the potential to meet the minimum graduation requirements and her skill makes her more attractive than other students whose academic credentials place them on the borderline for admission.

The more competitive a college is for admission, the more significant the talent must be to influence an admissions decision. How the level of significance is determined is based upon the priorities of the college. Most colleges and universities, at all selectivity levels, will have an interest in athletes. Regardless of the school's athletic division, if it has an athletic program, there will be student athletes in whom coaches are interested in order to strengthen their programs. College faculty and staff in other areas can also influence admissions decisions. Students with particular talent and skill in the visual or performing arts may also benefit from faculty interest.

No matter what the nature of a student's talent, if there is hope that it will develop into something significant enough to be part of your child's college search process, it will most likely be important to foster it over a period of years. Parents of middle schoolers will likely have an idea of whether or not their child is particularly gifted in athletics, music, art, whatever. If you discover a strength and a similar level of proclivity for the activity by your child, be sure to support her in her endeavors and offer her the means accessible to you to develop her skills to her potential.

In the case of athletic talent (see below), college coaches will scout student-athletes at premier sports camps and at the invitation of their high school coaches. Elite athletes will be wooed by many college coaches and may find the extra attention both flattering and nerve-wracking. In many cases, college coaches are able to meet their recruits and see them play in person. They call, write, and invite the students they hope to welcome onto their team to campus for visits to meet with current players and experience life as an athlete at their college even for just a day. The attention to students with talents in other areas is not nearly as intense but can have the same effect. Artistically talented students will most likely not be wined and dined in the same manner as athletes, but they will also have the opportunity to showcase their talent. Visual and performing artists will have the opportunity to submit a portfolio or audition that may be reviewed by admissions officers and faculty members within the discipline of interest. Parents of younger students can help their artistically talented children prepare for potential college auditions and portfolios by exposing them to performance opportunities at an early age. As with anything, the more comfortable a student is in a setting, even one that might be intimidating, the better she is likely to perform.

Athletics and College Admissions

Although issues surrounding collegiate athletics will not be pertinent until your child reaches high school, being familiar with the regulations concerning them and the recruitment process on a basic level can be helpful to the parents of younger students. The NCAA, or National Collegiate Athletic Association, is the governing body of college sports. The NCAA is the body responsible for policing collegiate sports, making sure that established guidelines are met. These rules are in place to ensure equity and fair play as well as protect the interest of student-athletes. High school athletes who hope to play at the collegiate level also come under the jurisdiction of the NCAA. There are academic standards that must be met by high school students who want to play collegiate sports. These regulations are in place to ensure that colleges recruit students who are capable of meeting the academic expectations of higher education. Additionally, there are guidelines that coaches and students must follow throughout the recruitment process. For instance, collegiate coaches are limited regarding when and the means by which they can communicate with recruited athletes. These regulations are in place in order to avoid undue stress and pressure on the student-athlete. If you are the parent of a talented athlete, be sure to visit the NCAA web site at *www.ncaa.org* to familiarize yourself with the regulations and guidelines surrounding collegiate athletics at all levels.

NCAA Divisions

Within the NCAA, there are three athletic divisions: Division I, Division II, and Division III. Because scholarships are awarded only by Division I and Division II schools, sometimes families believe Division III programs are not competitive. While certainly it is not likely that a Division III football program will ever appear in a postseason bowl game, that does not mean the program is not high quality and competitive within its league.

Most of the nation's high-profile athletic programs are Division I. Large schools, such as the University of Michigan and Penn State, sponsor Division I athletic programs. But smaller colleges such as Boston College and Fordham University also offer programs at this level. The size of the university is not the determining factor in what NCAA division it competes. It is the school's philosophy on athletics and its place in the life of its student-athletes that determines what division meets the needs of the institution. The key for student-athletes and their parents to remember is that athletic talent can have an impact on admission at schools of any NCAA division, but only colleges in Divisions I and II can offer scholarships for students who perform at an elite level.

While your child's talent level will determine in large part which NCAA Division is appropriate, families certainly make the final determination about which type of program is best suited for the student's goals. A student-athlete, for instance, who wants to pursue a degree such as engineering or biology, which requires significant lab work or heavy credit loads, may decide that the hectic travel schedule of a Division I program is not compatible with her academic goals. Such obligations may conflict often with academic requirements and would likely hinder scholastic efforts. Obviously, there are travel requirements for students who compete at Division III schools, but the distances between league schools may be smaller and/or there may be fewer games scheduled, or they might be limited to weekends.

Parents must remember that there are strict regulations and standards in place for both student and coach behavior during the college search process. Parents and students must make the effort to familiarize themselves with the NCAA rules governing student action in order to conduct an ethical search that will not lead to their disqualification from the process. A student's high school coach or guidance counselor will be a valuable source of information about this and other aspects of the college search and should be relied upon for direction.

Visual and Performing Arts

While visual and performing artists don't generally get the same attention that athletes do, without a weekend day devoted to television coverage of their efforts or a full month of madness each year covering the culmination of their efforts, they might also receive some assistance in the admissions process as a result of their innate talent and skill. It may, however, be more difficult to find colleges and universities that routinely recognize strength in these areas, unlike athletics, which is quite prevalent.

One of the first decisions an artist must make is whether or not she will attend a college or university that offers a full complement of courses and programs of study or a conservatory. There is a dramatic difference between the graduation requirements and even the admissions procedures between these two types of schools so deciding early which is preferred can be very beneficial. Students who choose to major in a visual or performing art in a department within a larger university setting will have to satisfy graduation requirements in their major as well as the broader graduation requirements all students at the school must meet in order to earn their degree. These requirements will likely fall in a broad range of areas, allowing a student to concentrate in one particular area of study but also requiring some exposure to other disciplines. Conservatory programs, even those that exist within a larger college or university setting, will have graduation requirements that focus heavily, if not solely, in the arts. There may be a handful of non-arts-related courses required but in general, students in these types of programs will be allowed to focus heavily on their area of interest and talent. Typically, the degree earned in each type of program differs as well. Students who study visual or performing arts within a larger university setting will often earn a Bachelor of Arts degree, while students at conservatories earn degrees such as the Bachelor of Fine Arts.

Considering Both Types of Programs

Parents of particularly talented younger children will find it helpful to consider both types of programs in order to be prepared for either option when the time comes. Students who apply to colleges and universities that are not conservatories will most likely have few talent-related regulations regarding their application process. They also most likely will find that their talent plays a smaller role in their admissions decision than if they apply to a conservatory. There are freestanding conservatories, such as the Juilliard School, and there are conservatories that are part of a larger university system, such as the Peabody Institute of Johns Hopkins University.

Students applying to conservatories of either type will find that their admission rests largely on the results of their portfolio or audition. While the academic credentials are considered, because the primary focus of a conservatory is artistic training, the student's record and abilities in other areas are less important.

Importance of the Academic Record

Although a candidate's academic record might be less important in the admission process of a conservatory program, parents should not assume that this decreased emphasis means the school is not competitive for admission—in fact, the opposite is true. In many cases, the nation's top conservatory programs have lower acceptance rates than many of the most competitive and best-known colleges and universities. In order to present herself in the best light, an applicant to a conservatory must have a significant portfolio or body of work in her repertoire. There will often be specific guidelines applicants must follow with regard to the required portfolio or audition. The earlier a student knows this type of school is appropriate for her and her goals, the better she can prepare for the rigorous application process she will face to gain admission.

Is Talent Enough to Earn a Scholarship?

Talent of any kind—academic, athletic, or artistic—can bring a student success in the admissions process and also in the search for funding to pay for college. It is important to understand the difference between the terms "scholarship" and "financial assistance" as you begin to consider college options for a particularly talented child.

Scholarships

Scholarship generally means a financial award given to a student with significant talent in one area without regard to the financial status of the student. Not all colleges and universities will offer scholarships although a vast majority offer financial assistance.

Financial Assistance

Financial assistance refers to the range of sources of funding a college or university makes available to a student to cover the cost of her attendance. It may include non-need-based components but will also most likely include need-based factors.

In the case of any type of merit award, the more appealing a student is within the applicant pool of the school to which she has applied, the more likely it is that she will receive a scholarship. Families that must make merit-based financial aid a determining factor in their college search will need to include a number of schools at which their child is stronger than most of the applicants in order to maximize the chances for receiving a scholarship. In the case of academic scholarships, to be successful in receiving one a student will most likely need to be at the top of the applicant pool, exceeding the average credentials of those admitted by quite a bit. For other types of scholarships, athletic, musical, artistic, theatrical, and so on, it is quite difficult to predict who will be a competitive candidate. Parents and students will need to research each school and scholarship to determine if it is well suited.

Are Activities a Means to Admission or Fun for Life?

When our children are young, it is easy to picture them in the future as anything our mind can imagine. The best player on the T-ball team becomes the next World Series' MVP. The master finger painter is destined to have a one-woman show at New York's finest galleries. The truth of the matter though is that a child who is particularly successful or remarkably talented in the early and middle grades may not continue to achieve at the same level as she grows and develops. Physical changes can affect athletic and even musical success. A child who is a standout at a young age may not continue to develop at a rate faster than her peers. One who once outperformed all the others may now find herself finishing near the bottom.

Parents of a talented child want to do whatever they can to foster their child's interests and abilities. Some parents, unfortunately, begin grooming their children for college-level recognition and participation at a very young age. Parents who do this risk having their child burn out, feel pressured, or develop a feeling of inadequacy if she doesn't live up to her own or her parents' expectations. It is important to remember that children enjoy a variety of activities and it is this enjoyment that should be encouraged. Children who are able to uncover and pursue interests are likely to continue trying new things and contributing to their communities, making them a valuable and integral member of them.

The middle school years, as students are beginning to gain a better understanding of who they are and what is important to them, are a wonderful time for experimentation and exposure to different activities. Remembering to allow the child to exert her preferences, parents should make one of their goals for this time introducing their children to a range of activities so that any undiscovered gifts and interests can be found. Doing so during the middle school years is beneficial because anything a student becomes interested in can be pursued and developed from these early years on through high school and beyond. As it is important for a child to develop a solid academic foundation in middle school, it is also valuable for her to begin discovering her personal likes and dislikes, discerning what is important to her and to what she wants to devote herself. This foundation may serve her well throughout life as the older we get and the more obligations and responsibilities we take on keep us from trying new things. Interests and hobbies we can carry with us from a young age, therefore, serve an important purpose; your child will be thankful you encouraged her interests and talents.

QUESTIONS TO ASK

- What does my child enjoy?
- What are my child's natural talents and abilities?
- Does my child have any particular strengths?
- Does my child have any areas of weakness that might be augmented by participating in a particular activity?
- What resources are available in my community to foster my child's interests and skills?

A CHECKLIST FOR HEALTHY AND FUN EXTRACURRICULAR INVOLVEMENT

- ❑ Check with your child's teacher or coach to see if your perception of her skill level is accurate.
- ❑ Determine some potential areas of interest of your child and look for local programs in which to participate.
- ❑ Try new activities as a family.
- ❑ Model commitment and participation for your child by continuing and sharing your own interests.

Chapter 7

Summer

A Day at the Beach or Fun with the Future in Mind?

Most kids and more than a few parents look forward to summer. Even after our own calendar no longer follows that of the school year, affording us three carefree months, we look forward to the summer months because everything seems to slow down a bit and many families find some time to get away and enjoy each other's company. As children get a little older, summer can bring some exciting opportunities that aren't feasible during the school year. From day camps to volunteer programs, kids can explore interests and develop talents of all kinds during the summer. It is important, however, to remember the intrinsic value of summer for children—the chance to slow down and relax, hopefully allowing their creativity and imagination to flourish.

Summer Programs

Many children participate in summer programs of some type from even an early age. If you decide that you would like your child to participate in something beyond the local community day camp, there are many options available, most likely even locally. As in any program you consider for your child, there are many factors to consider, not the least of which is why it might be beneficial to your child.

There are many types of summer programs; some have a very specific focus, but many are very broad in their offerings. These more general programs tend to include arts and crafts, physical activities, games, and field trips. They are great for young children and provide wonderful opportunities for social interaction and growth.

Summer Camp

A camp experience, like school, can be a great time for your child to develop some essential personal qualities that can be especially helpful as he grows into adulthood. This personal development can be as important a reason for choosing to send your child to camp as any of his skills or talents you hope will strengthen or improve. At camp, whether day camp or sleepaway, kids can learn some important skills and become self-reliant as a result of taking responsibility for themselves.

When your child went off to school for the first time, he had to take care of some of his basic needs on his own, without Mom or Dad to put on his coat, keep track of a hat, or figure out what to do when. Obviously, teachers of these youngest students are patient men and women who help children learn these skills, but eventually, over the course of the school year, children learn how to get along on their own in a school setting. Many summer experiences can do the same thing for children of any age, affording the opportunity to learn social skills that will last a lifetime.

Childhood Friendships

Many early childhood friendships are formed out of convenience for the parents. Children of couples who are friends often play together and build their child's first social circle. Day care or preschool provide the setting for developing a larger social circle, but still one that is somewhat limited by circumstances. Kindergarten, generally a larger setting than preschool or day care, allows children to interact with a broader range of kids and to make more social choices for themselves. Unless a family moves or lives in an area that is relatively transient, children move through elementary school with mostly the same kids. The move to middle school or junior high school is one of the first times children are forced to interact with many new students. Some children will handle this transition well; others will not. Whether your child managed this change well or not, a summer camp experience will provide more practice making friends and adapting to a new social situation that is beneficial for everyone.

Independence

One of the most powerful feelings for anyone is that of independence. Certainly, most parents aren't too anxious for their middle schooler to be *very* independent, but most recognize the value of it. Even in children, a sense of independence brings a sense of empowerment that gives them confidence in themselves and the decisions they make. As important as the content children learn in school or in other settings is, learning to make their own decisions and to be comfortable with their own values is even more so. While it may seem a long way from attending a summer camp to making good life and personal decisions, being on his own in a secure and safe setting such as a camp, and realizing he can manage it, can be an initial step toward independence.

Personal Responsibility

One of the biggest tasks parents face is instilling in their children a sense of personal responsibility and the ability to take care of themselves. Parents make tremendous headway in this area before children even enter kindergarten, and teachers help continue the effort. Summer camp, even a day camp, can provide continued practice in self-reliance for a child. In some circumstances, camps may provide less adult support for children so they must take more initiative and responsibility. Children, then, can continue to practice taking care of themselves by keeping track of their items, following a schedule, and monitoring their actions at camp.

Check Out the Camp Program

Once you've decided that you would like your child to attend a summer program or camp, there are practical but very important things to consider beyond what your child will gain from the experience. Among these factors are the camp's accreditation and safety records, the schedule and duration, the owners, and whether or not you can afford the program. As with anything parents consider for their children, safety is paramount. We will often check references for contractors who come into our homes for various improvement projects, and it is equally important to maintain a similar level of scrutiny for those who teach or interact with our children. When investigating a camp or summer program, be sure to request references and follow up with them. It may also be beneficial to research the program on the Web or contact your area's Better Business Bureau. Parents should look for safety and health violations as well as any reports of injury or neglect to children.

Who sponsors or funds a camp can be important if those who do promote certain ideological, political, or religious views that conflict with yours. It is important for parents to investigate the management and/or ownership of the summer programs they are considering for their children. In some cases the ideals of a sponsor may have no or very little impact on the summer program offered, but parents need to be certain that if it is doctrine-based they agree with what is being taught.

Cost

Once you've determined that a camp is safe and appropriate for your child, you need to figure out if it is feasible for you based upon cost, schedule, and duration. For working parents, covering the cost of summer programs is a fact of life. That doesn't mean, however, that the sky's the limit. For anyone considering a summer camp for their child, cost is an important consideration in addition to convenience. It may, for instance, be worth a certain amount extra per week for a summer program that offers "before" and "after" care programs, making it more convenient for a parent's work schedule. Other programs, more conveniently located to a parent's work or home may be more appealing as commuting time is not extended. Some parents might want a program that will last the full summer, making scheduling a little easier as both adult and child can adjust to one place, one staff, and one routine. Others may value diversity of experience and not mind a changing routine. As a parent, determine what consideration is most important to you and look for programs that meet it.

For some families, the cost of summer programs may be prohibitive even if they are necessary. In such cases, there may be some financial assistance available. While such aid may not be widely available, some government-funded programs or those that recognize special talents or skills may offer some assistance to particularly needy or able children. The cost of finding out whether aid is available is relatively small, usually a phone call or review of a web site, and can lead to a valuable experience for your child.

The Options

Depending on your child's age, there are many, many options available to you for the summer. There are traditional day camps and sleepaway camps, precollege programs, sports camps, arts programs, interest-based camps, volunteer opportunities, and employment programs. Obviously, younger children will have fewer options from which to choose, but as your child approaches and enters high school, the range of opportunities will broaden and include many appealing and impressive choices.

Traditional Summer Camps

Many parents harbor fond memories of summer because of their camp experiences. Whether their vacation months were spent at a residential summer program or merely heading off each morning to a local YMCA or community center and returning at night, the friendships made and traditions learned are what make camp memories so enduring. Parents who have such memories want to offer their children the same experience. Those parents who never had this experience but have learned of it from friends or other sources want to offer their kids something they weren't afforded. Regardless of the motivation of the parents, summer camps can provide children with wonderful opportunities for fun and personal development.

Other Programs

If your child is too young for a sleepaway or residential camp, your options are limited to programs near your home. Finding such a program can be as easy as a review of your local phone book. As in all areas, the Internet can also be a powerful search tool. In many communities, there are parenting publications that contain annual overviews of local summer programs. Similar reviews may appear in local newspapers and other publications. In metropolitan areas, there may be summer camp fairs and information sessions that allow parents to speak directly with camp personnel, a great way to begin investigating different program options. Your child's school may also be a useful source of information about summer camps as well as a sponsor of one. It's not always necessary to stray far from the familiar to find a worthwhile program, and such surroundings may be beneficial to your child. Regardless of whether you choose a program at a site your child knows well or one new to him, surveying the many choices available to him will likely uncover many that are appropriate.

If you are able to consider an overnight camp for your child, you need to consider how far from home you are comfortable sending him. It could be that you attended a residential program as a child and you'd like your child to have the same experience, even if it means sending him to a camp a distance from home. Your comfort zone, however, may be more limited. Whatever your geographic limitations, there are likely many programs you can consider that will be appealing.

Colleges and universities are often sites of summer camps. For high school students, college campuses can offer a broad range of opportunities from precollege programs to subject-specific camps such as yearbook and newspaper camps. For younger students, colleges may offer camps of a broader nature. Camps on college campuses can offer terrific opportunities, allowing students to experience life away from home, exposure to state-of-the-art facilities, and interaction with all types of people, including the counselors who will most likely be students at the college and can become role models for younger kids. If there is a college or university near you that has summer camps, it may offer you the best of both worlds, a residential experience that isn't too far from home.

Specialty Camps

There are many types of specialty camps where students can hone skills and talents, ranging from the visual arts to foul shots. Whatever your child's strengths, finding a camp to suit him is most likely just a Web search away. Unlike summer camps with a broader focus, finding a program with a specialized curriculum may mean that you need to consider sites in a wider range of locations and programs that are residential in nature. If your child is relatively young, you may not be comfortable sending him away, even for a high-caliber experience. As he gets older, though, you may become more comfortable with the idea of him attending a program away from you, so considering such programs early on may allow you to find something appealing for when the time becomes appropriate.

Fine and Performing Arts

There are programs throughout the country that offer topflight instruction and guidance in the fine and performing arts. Some, such as Interlochen Arts Camp in Interlochen, Michigan, have international reputations for exceptional staff and attracting high-caliber students. The alumni of such programs include some of today's most successful practitioners in the field. Not all students have access to such programs, however, and fortunately there are many other camps for all ability levels.

Regardless of the profile of the arts camp in which you are interested or your child attends, one of the best features of attending such a program is the opportunity for your child to be surrounded by peers with interests similar to his own. For a child who has the inklings of a passion in the arts, time spent in an environment that immerses him in his field of interest is the experience of a lifetime. Within the realm of fine and performing arts camps, there are programs that focus on more traditional forms of performing or visual arts, such as dance, instrumental music, and theater, and there are others that focus on such things as film production, photography, and computer graphics.

Sports Camps

As with budding artists, there are camps that allow kids to hone their athletic talents. Sports camps, like traditional summer camps, may be more prevalent and easily accessible, however, providing parents with more options. There are sports camps that cater to young children, focusing on basic skills in order to build a foundation. While there are age considerations for participation, children may be at beginner skill levels. There are other sports camps, however, that are designed only for children who possess a high level of talent. Such camps may serve as scouting events for college coaches and generally require an invitation or recommendation from a coach for participation. For athletes at this level of play, it is important to time participation in them appropriately to allow for maximum exposure. Generally, the summer prior to the student's senior year of high school is a key time for exposure to collegiate coaches.

Academically Focused Programs

There are summer programs available that are geared to particularly bright children. The CTY, or Center for Talented Youth, based at Johns Hopkins University in Baltimore, Maryland, is probably the best-known program for gifted children. This program is for students of middle school age; admission is competitive and is based upon a student's performance on the SAT I. Children who attend CTY and other programs designed for intellectually gifted children are surrounded, maybe for the first time, by kids equally talented and, as a result, are able to be exposed to academic issues at a higher level than they might normally be able to be in their typical educational setting. Such interaction and exposure can be very stimulating and can motivate a child in a way they aren't in other settings. It may help a child find educational motivation to succeed in order to allow himself access to a similar kind of collegiate experience.

Summer Activities for High School Students

Although the programs discussed below are suitable primarily for high school students, because some are accessible to students in the early years of high school, it is beneficial that they be included here.

Counselor in Training (CIT) Programs

In some cases, students and parents don't need to look further than their own summer camp experience for a valuable summer opportunity. Many camps use teens in the capacity of "counselors in training" to staff their programs. Students in this capacity will not have full or unsupervised responsibility for campers but will be very involved in the day-to-day operations of the camp, working with children often in an area of specialty for the CIT. As a "teacher" of sorts, this opportunity allows the student to fine-tune his own skills in a specialty as he will be required to share his knowledge with others, learning about his own abilities in the process. Because he will be responsible for the activities and routine of a particular group of campers, he will also have the chance to begin or continue developing his leadership skills. While leading a group of children in a summer program is an important responsibility and one that can be surprisingly intimidating, most who have served in this role probably feel it was a friendly and warm training ground for leadership skills. The skills learned in such an environment, those of organization, responsibility, and the ability to motivate and influence people, are tremendously valuable and very transferable. Acquiring such strengths can be viewed as equally valuable as any monetary compensation a counselor in training program might offer.

Precollege Programs

Once students have completed their first year of high school, many academically oriented summer programs sponsored by colleges and universities become accessible to them. These programs, while having a variety of titles, can fall into the category of precollege programs. They serve as an introduction to the collegiate experience, allowing teens to live in a college residence hall under the supervision of a Resident Advisor employed by the college. There will be social activities in which the student can participate as well as appropriate structure and expectations for behavior in order to ensure the students' safety. The main attraction of precollege programs, however, is academic in nature. Students will enroll in courses offered by the college. These courses may be specifically designed for high school students in order to strengthen or enrich academic skills, or they may be the actual summer course offerings available to those students who are enrolled in the school's degree programs. Regardless of which type of courses the precollege program offers, the experience of sitting in a college classroom, interacting with college professors and potentially even current college students can be a powerful intellectual experience. If you would like to consider a precollege program for your child, you might investigate whether a local college or university offers one or find out if your own alma mater has any opportunities for high school students. In both cases, the college setting will likely be somewhat familiar and, therefore, less intimidating and more comfortable for your child.

Most precollege programs limit students to enrollment in one or two courses. Under these circumstances, unlike their regular school schedule, students are able to focus greater attention and effort on the subjects they are studying, gaining greater depth of understanding. Such programs also focus on helping students develop some of the foundation skills necessary for future academic success. Programs may be writing-intensive or require significant in-class participation. Possessing such skills in high school will bring greater academic success during those years and beyond.

Precollege programs designed to enhance specific academic skills or address particular weaknesses are available as well. There are study skills programs that teach students effective note taking, exam review, and research habits. There are programs that focus on SAT preparation, and still others that target weak writing skills. A program such as these may be beneficial to your child if he is experiencing academic difficulty during the school year but may not be able to fit tutoring or programs in this area into his schedule at that time. As is the case in precollege programs that offer courses in more traditional college subject matter, the opportunity for a child to focus on his studies in one area without the distraction and dilution of effort of many courses may be especially beneficial.

Regardless of what type of precollege program you consider for your child, there are many benefits. As in the case of sending a younger child to a day camp program where he is responsible for himself and his belongings, an older child who has the opportunity to live away from home, even for a short time, doing things as seemingly mundane as laundry and getting to a dining hall for meals, can find such an experience particularly empowering. A child who is successful meeting his own needs will feel a wonderful sense of independence and confidence that can pay big dividends when he returns home and gets back to his normal high school routine.

Special Interest Programs

As is the case with more traditional summer camp programs available to younger children, there is a very broad range of summer opportunities open to high school students. These programs, sponsored by civic organizations, government bodies, and other privately sponsored agencies can offer wonderful opportunities for students. Remember, as is the case when investigating summer camps for younger children, it is important to consider the safety efforts and record of the program as well as its appropriateness and feasibility for you and your child. Some of the programs available to high school students are extremely worthwhile but they also carry a hefty price tag. This expense may be one you can easily afford but it may not, and it is important to determine whether or not it is financially feasible for your child. For parents who might not be able to offer their children the opportunity to participate in an expensive, seemingly prestigious summer program, they should be reassured that the lack of such participation on their child's résumé will not limit future college options. It is also important to remember that there are many meaningful opportunities available that have little or no cost associated with them. In many instances, these activities may even be more impressive to the individuals your child encounters in the college admissions process and beyond.

For those families who are interested, there are a tremendous number of special interest programs available. Many special interest programs offer insight into our nation's government and its broad sphere of influence. Such programs, often (understandably) based in Washington, D.C., can draw students from around the country and even the world, providing a wonderful blend of perspectives and experiences from which your child can learn. Programs such as the Presidential

Classroom, Boys' and Girls' Nation, and those offered by the National Youth Leadership Forum, just to name a few, bring students with similar interests together to interact with government officials and discuss issues facing our country today. Whatever your child's area of interest, a quick Web search will produce a long list of potential summer programs to meet his needs.

Another area of summer program based on special interest is outdoor skills and leadership programs. Organizations such as Outward Bound and National Outdoor Leadership School (NOLS) are leaders in the field of outdoor education. Programs range from those that teach sailing and water survival skills to those that deal with rock climbing and techniques for existing in the wild. These types of programs are geared toward students with an interest in the outdoors and a desire to test themselves against nature. Other students find themselves enrolled in an outdoor education program because they have encountered difficulties in their own home or school environment. Time spent in nature allows students to reflect and gain a broader perspective of their own lives. Students often grow to appreciate where they came from in addition to the wonders of nature as a result of an Outward Bound or NOLS program. Often, though, the most important outcome of such a program is the dramatically increased sense of confidence and belief in oneself that is developed as a result of having to rely solely on one's own physical capabilities and resourcefulness. Whatever the reason an outdoor experience might be appealing, few who complete them remain unchanged as a result of the experience.

Study Abroad Programs

In today's increasingly global economy and shrinking world, any opportunity for a child to become more knowledgeable about different cultures and other parts of the world should be viewed as particularly worthwhile and valuable. Although American children who grow up in many parts of the United States are often exposed to a wide range of cultures, languages, and traditions in their own communities, the experience of traveling outside our country and immersing oneself in another culture altogether can prove to be a life-altering experience. For parents, the thought of sending a child beyond the boundaries of our country might be intimidating at best, terrifying at worst. If, however, you are a parent who can balance the value of this kind of experience with some of the risks involved, you may find that your child benefits tremendously from the experience, and you might just get a great vacation out of it as well. Again, as is the case with any type of program, a primary responsibility of parents is to be certain the program their child participates in is safe, appropriate, and reputable. Gathering and checking references should be particularly important for families considering study abroad programs.

Study abroad programs can be affiliated with a U.S. college, university, or high school. They may also be sponsored by organizations that specialize in such programs. There are some programs that are immersion in nature, requiring the student to live and speak as a full member of the community and culture he is visiting. These programs may include a home-stay component through which the student will live with a local family, experiencing life as a native of the country. Others will house students in dormitory or group living situations that will allow them to live with others participating in the program. As a family, you will need to determine which type of setting is best for the student. Often, this decision will help determine which study abroad programs are appropriate and feasible.

There are also study abroad programs that are not immersion-based. They may allow a student to study an area of interest in an English-speaking country or to learn the country's language at a less intensive level of an immersion program. For instance, a student may study art in Italy or theater in France in a situation that is similar to studying those subjects in an American setting. The instructors will speak English and the students will attend classes or lectures in their native language. They may not have significant contact with those who live in the area surrounding their program's base. While an emphasis may not be placed on learning the language of the host country and students may not have the opportunity to experience the local culture in depth, such an experience can still be very worthwhile to a student and can spark an interest in either the subject studied or learning about cultures other than his own.

Most colleges and universities encourage students to study abroad at some point during their undergraduate years. Many schools sponsor their own programs in other countries, and most others allow students to participate in programs offered by other schools, granting credit for courses completed and even, in some cases, factoring grades earned into the student's GPA. As the need for Americans to better understand the world around them grows, international experiences have become particularly valuable and impressive. A student who has had the chance to study abroad prior to enrolling in college will have a perspective that is welcomed and valued.

Volunteer Programs

As is the case in many circumstances, the flashiest or most expensive experience or program is not always the best. Certainly there is value in many kinds of summer programs that carry a hefty price tag, but for those who can't afford such programs or who choose not to pursue them, there are plenty of opportunities that expand the perspective of a child and offer great rewards. Community service and volunteer programs are such opportunities as they allow a child to give of himself and experience the satisfaction such action can bring. Of course the point of community service and volunteer efforts is not what it can do for the person volunteering but rather what it can do for those he is assisting.

Schools, hospitals, community organizations, and local and state agencies are great resources for volunteer opportunities. A simple Web search or a review of your local phone book will likely yield a listing of organizations that can use volunteers. Before blindly calling or visiting potential volunteer sites, however, it will be helpful to consider your child's personality and interests. A child who is squeamish around those who are ill, for instance, might not be the best candidate for a position at a hospital; that same child, though, may love animals and might enjoy participating in a pet therapy program at a local assisted living facility. Taking care to help your child pick a site where he will feel comfortable will increase the likelihood of a successful volunteer experience.

While many organizations will prefer to have older children as volunteers, there are many that will also welcome family groups. It may be, therefore, that you can introduce your child to the benefits of volunteering even when he is young if you choose to participate as well. As all parents know, we are the first role models for our children, and what better example to set than that of a volunteer. Participating in family volunteer programs sponsored by your school, church, or synagogue is a great first step in fostering a sense of empathy and civic responsibility in your child.

Summer Jobs

For some families meeting the financial needs of everyday modern life may be a considerable challenge. It's possible that children old enough to work must do so in order to cover the costs of some of their expenses. It may also be that a child simply wants to work in order to feel self-reliant or to gain experience within a particular field of interest. Whatever the reason a student may choose to work, a summer job can provide very valuable lessons in responsibility, commitment, and managing one's money and time.

If your child is interested in working in the summer, the commitment may not be only his to assume. Teens who don't yet drive, for instance, may need to rely on you for transportation. Children may also need to rely on parents to get up on time for work and to help them manage their other activities. Before allowing your child to take on a summer job of any kind, be sure it is a time commitment your family can afford to meet.

A first summer job, whether it is a regular baby-sitting job or lawn care for a neighbor, is an important step in a child learning the meaning of commitment and time management. By their very nature, children and teens are self-centered and not always able to see how their actions impact others. A person at this stage of development may not realize on his own that the neighbor who has arranged an important meeting for a specific time and secured his services as a baby-sitter might be tremendously inconvenienced if the sitter arrives even just 15 minutes late. As difficult as it may be, it is important for parents of first-time employees to help them understand that sometimes meeting the demands of a commitment may require some sacrifice of personal time and fun with friends. It may mean that your child has to forego a fun activity or event, but helping him learn this important lesson at an early age will be very valuable as he grows and takes on greater responsibility. To instill this lesson, parents cannot "bail" their children out when meeting a commitment means making a tough choice or sacrifice. Initially, the lesson may hurt, but in the end the student will be the winner as he will gain the satisfaction intrinsic in a job well done.

The summer may be an ideal time for a student to seek employment, and while some may want to continue working into the school year, parents should be cautioned about allowing them to do so. A school-year job should be allowed only if the child can meet the expectations of school, family, and work without undue strain. As with any school-year activity, a job can provide valuable structure and help a child develop strong time management skills. As with any other activity, however, if the demands of the job begin to negatively impact grades or other commitments, parents should decide whether to allow the child to continue working, for although a job can bring significant benefits to the child, a teenager's primary duty in most cases is doing well in school, and no activity should infringe on that responsibility.

Checking Out Summer Programs

As is the case with any activity a child is involved with, a summer program is beneficial to him only if he actually wants to participate and actively engages in it. Summer programs of any kind should be considered only if the child has a sincere desire to be involved, not because parents think it would look good on an activity sheet when the time comes to apply for college. As with anything in life, a child will get out of something what he puts in, and if all that is put in is the check for the program's registration, little will be gained by anyone.

No matter how appealing some of these options may be, there are some families for whom they may not be appropriate. Children who have experienced academic difficulty during the school year might need to enroll in remediation courses during the summer. While this proposal is not likely to inspire great excitement in either student or parent, it should be taken seriously. As is the case for students who enroll in summer programs for enrichment, the opportunity to focus full effort on an area of weakness can be equally powerful. Because middle school is the time to develop a strong academic foundation in order to achieve success in high school, any opportunity to strengthen a child's scholastic base, whether during the school year or summer, should be exploited.

If you have decided a summer program may be fun and meaningful to your child, there are many resources to which you can refer to find the ones that might be most appealing. There are many printed resources to help you find a summer camp or program that is suitable for your child. The Web can be a powerful search tool as well, guiding parents to information about local summer camp fairs as well as to search engines to find specific programs. The following web sites may prove helpful to you as you begin your search.

1. American Camping Association—*www.acacamps.org*
2. Study Abroad—*www.studyabroad.com*

3. National Camp Association—*www.summercamp.org*
4. U.S. Sports and Specialty Camps—*www.ussportscamps.com*

As exciting as many of these options may be, parents and children will be well served if everyone remembers that the summer break from school has intrinsic value and purpose all on its own. In today's over-scheduled family life, taking advantage of the slower pace of summer is something parents should make a priority. Children, like adults, need some downtime to become rejuvenated and refreshed. Some unscheduled, unstructured time can provide valuable time to reflect, create, and imagine, many of the best things childhood allows.

QUESTIONS TO ASK

- Can we afford a summer camp or special interest program for our child?
- What kind of program and setting are best for our child?
- What do we hope our child will gain from a summer program?
- Does our child have any special interests or talents that could be enriched by a program that allows him to focus his time fully on endeavors in this area?
- Does our child have any weaknesses or deficiencies that would be well served by an intensive study program, focusing on these areas?
- Will our family's schedule accommodate a summer program?

A CHECKLIST FOR SUMMER

❑ Survey friends, relatives, and coworkers for suggestions of summer programs they have completed and found worthwhile.
❑ Ask school personnel for listings of summer opportunities that may be appropriate for your child.
❑ Ask your child's teacher or counselor if she would recommend a summer program of any type to address any relative strengths or weaknesses.

❏ Research summer opportunities, requesting references and information about program, schedule, and activities.
❏ Watch for reviews of summer camps in local newspapers and community publications.
❏ Search for information about summer camp fairs in your area.

Chapter 8

College Planning for Students with Learning Differences

ven when she sleeps, your child is in constant motion, pillows and blankets everywhere. It seems that whatever keeps her foot tapping, head bobbing, and pencil fidgeting during the day doesn't rest, even at night. Such is the life of a child (and her parents) with AD/HD. Whether your child has been diagnosed with Attention Deficit/Hyperactivity Disorder (AD/HD) or a processing-related learning disability, chances are you have already had to educate yourselves about the appropriate learning environment for your child. The college search process for your child will be tailored to include consideration of her learning profile as well. The most important thing for parents to keep in mind is that the college search for a student with learning disabilities must take into account the student's individual learning needs and required support services in addition to the more general criteria all students and families must consider when embarking on the college search.

Accepting the Diagnosis

Before a family can begin to consider the appropriate learning environment for a child's college years, they must come to grips with the reality of the child's disabilities, no matter how mild or severe. Depending on the view of learning disabilities within a family's community, the student and parents may feel there is a stigma attached to the diagnosis of one.

Others, however, will be fortunate and will live in a community that is educated and has the information and services able to meet the needs of the child. Regardless of what type of environment you live in, it is imperative for the parents of a child with a diagnosed learning disability to help their child understand her learning needs and to recognize her relative weaknesses and strengths. Remembering that there are inherent strengths in all learning types, even in the face of learning disabilities, will prove invaluable in preserving a child's self-esteem. Self-esteem is a key ingredient in a student's academic success and her well-being in general. Parents must help their child to develop and maintain a solid foundation of self-worth even as she learns about her learning disability and how it makes her different from her peers.

As students with different types of disabilities will need different services from a college in order to succeed, colleges will have varying levels and types of services for students with learning disabilities. It is essential that parents and students know the appropriate level of support and how to find out whether or not the colleges they are considering offer it. The first step in knowing whether or not a college can meet your child's needs is knowing what those needs are. It is imperative that both the parent and the student understand the student's learning style and accept it. Only after the student and parents have assessed and defined the needs of the student with learning disabilities can a meaningful college search begin.

Learning Disabilities—A Diagnosis

As unusual as it may sound, the earlier a student is diagnosed with a learning disability, the better. As is the case with a physical concern, the earlier a diagnosis is made and treatment begun, the earlier the individual can begin to recover from the illness or injury. Unlike a physical ailment, however, a learning disability is not something a student generally "recovers" from. Rather, a student learns to accommodate for the disability in order to reach her own academic potential. As the treatment of a physical condition will vary, so will the coping mechanisms employed by a child with learning disabilities. Again, the earlier a student is diagnosed with a learning disability, the earlier treatment can begin and, subsequently, the earlier the student can begin to acquire successfully the academic foundation on which later school success will be based. For example, a student with undiagnosed and therefore untreated AD/HD is missing information throughout the school day during periods of distraction. If the student is intellectually able, she may be able to find academic success for quite some time without difficulty, achieving because even with "holes" in her foundation, she is bright enough to get most of the information needed to do well on assignments and tests. Unfortunately, however, this type of student is the one who may ultimately suffer the most as she will be able to "hide" her AD/HD for quite some time, missing information for many years. By the time the condition is diagnosed, finding and making up for the weaknesses in the foundation can be very difficult. The same can be said for all types of learning disabilities that affect a student's ability to acquire information. If you are the parent of a child who you suspect of having, or who you've been asked to have evaluated for, a learning disability or AD/HD but haven't yet done so, you should, in order to help your child to continue or to begin achieving academic success.

Types of Learning Disabilities

There are many types of learning disabilities and many degrees of severity. Some children experience only one type of learning disability, while others may present symptoms of a combination of conditions. An individual treatment and accommodation plan is needed for each child and her unique profile. Because many parents have not been exposed to the field of learning disabilities until their child is diagnosed, it may be helpful to define the most common types of learning disabilities and their symptoms.

Learning disabilities can be divided into several categories. There are developmental speech and language disorders, academic skills disorders, and attention deficit disorders. Within each category there are distinct conditions and children can be diagnosed with one or a combination of them in varying levels of severity.

- *Developmental speech and language disorders* affect either a child's ability to receive information through aural or visual means or her ability to express herself.
- *Academic skills disorders* directly impact a student's ability to learn school-related skills such as reading and writing.
- *Dyslexia* is an academic skills disorder that hinders a student's ability to read because letters, words, and the sequences of both are not easily deciphered by the student.
- *Attention deficit disorders* impede a child's ability to regulate her attention and behavior. Some children with Attention Deficit Disorder or Attention Deficit/Hyperactivity Disorder (AD/HD) are quite impulsive, unable to control their physical and verbal actions. This behavior is not only disruptive to the classroom setting but the child is so distracted and unable to attend to the lesson that she misses much of what is being taught. Kids with ADD or AD/HD can easily be labeled as "problem" children when in fact their behavior, while disruptive, is not malicious.

Psychoeducational Evaluations

Often, a child's teacher is the first to notice behaviors or performance that indicate the existence of a learning disability. While personnel at a child's school will be important sources of information as she is evaluated for a learning disability, the actual diagnosis must come from a trained psychologist as a result of a comprehensive psychoeducational evaluation. A full evaluation will include not only a description of the condition that impact's the child's learning ability, but also recommendations about the appropriate educational environment for her and any accommodations that might be necessary and/or beneficial.

A good psychoeducational report includes many components. The first consideration, once you have decided your child needs to undergo an evaluation, is to determine who will examine her. The counselor at your child's school, the school's principal, or your child's pediatrician are your best resources as you begin to look for a professional to evaluate her. The individual you take your child to should have extensive training as well as significant experience working with children. Appropriate professionals to consider are: "clinical or educational psychologists; school psychologists; neuropsychologists; learning disabilities specialists; medical doctors with training and experience in the assessment of learning problems" according to the Educational Testing Service's Policy Statement for Documentation of a Learning Disability in Adolescents and Adults.

Once you've found a professional you are comfortable with and have confidence in, it is important to be sure that the report that will result from the consultation includes the information necessary to be helpful to you, your child, and her school in its efforts to serve her. Additionally, for high school students who plan to take standardized tests such as the PSAT, SAT I and II, AP exams, and the ACT, it is imperative that the evaluator's report include specific components in order to allow the student to qualify for accommodations. The College Board recommends the inclusion of the following information in a psychoeducational evaluation in order to fully inform the family of the child's learning profile and maximize the likelihood of accommodations being granted when it is time for standardized testing.

On the Services for Students with Disabilities section of the College Board's web site, the following documentation guidelines are outlined when a request for extended time and other accommodations is made.

The documentation must: 1. state the specific disability, as diagnosed; 2. be current (in most cases, the evaluation should be completed within three years of the request for accommodations); 3. provide relevant educational, developmental, and medical history; 4. describe the comprehensive testing and techniques used to arrive at the diagnosis (including evaluation date(s) and test results with subtest scores from measures of cognitive ability, current academic achievement, and information processing); 5. describe the functional limitations supported by the test results; 6. describe the specific accommodations requested, and state why the student's disability qualifies the student for such accommodations on standardized tests; and 7. establish the professional credentials of the evaluator, including information about license or certification and area of specialization.

If the accommodations requested do not include extended time, the documentation must outline the specific accommodations needed and the reason for them, and confirm that similar adjustments are made for in-school assignments and tests according to the College Board's web site. While the information noted above will be beneficial in securing accommodations on important standardized tests, once a student is in high school, its importance actually lies in the fact that it will allow the student, parents, and school to work together to create a learning environment that will maximize the student's potential.

Parents as Advocates

A thorough psychoeducational evaluation report is helpful to parents, but it cannot be fully beneficial to the child and her success until it is shared with the student's school. While families may be reluctant to share the information included in the psychoeducational evaluation because they fear some sort of stigma they perceive to be attached to the diagnosis of a learning disability, it is important to move beyond such feelings in order to allow the student to achieve appropriate success in school. One of the most important roles a parent of a child with learning disabilities can assume is that of advocate. As a child progresses through high school and on to college, it will be important for her to begin to become her own advocate, understanding her own needs and asking for the accommodations she needs. Parents of younger children, however, must take on this role for their child, petitioning her school, if necessary, for the appropriate services and accommodations. Being an effective advocate may mean that the parent needs to become a self-educated expert on the type of learning disability with which the child has been diagnosed. Parents should ask their school, pediatrician, and evaluator for readings and studies to learn more about their child's learning disability. There are also community-based resources, advocacy groups, and membership associations that can offer insight into the condition as well as support for parents and children.

Public Schools

- In a public school setting, students with documented learning disabilities who receive support in the school environment must have an IEP or Individualized Education Program under the Individuals with Disabilities Education Act or IDEA. This document, written by parents, teachers, and school officials, provides a plan for the student's education. It should include a description of the learning disability, what services the school can provide, goals for the student for the current school year, and where the student will learn. The IEP is reviewed and revised annually with parental involvement in the process.

- Another term all parents of children with learning disabilities will become familiar with is "Section 504." This term refers to Section 504 of the Rehabilitation Act of 1973, which requires that all individuals with learning disabilities are guaranteed certain rights and equal access to programs and services. Unlike the IDEA, however, Section 504 does not require the development of an IEP; generally, Section 504 does not offer as much protection for students and parents as the IDEA does.

Independent Schools

Independent schools, unlike public schools, are not required to meet the specific indications of the IDEA. Students in independent schools, if they are understanding and supportive of the needs of individuals with learning disabilities, will receive support and accommodations to enhance their learning experiences as a result of individual and tailored attention. In some cases, independent schools may, in fact, be able to better serve students with learning disabilities because they offer smaller class sizes and more individualized attention. In all settings, public or independent, it is important for parents of children with learning disabilities to understand what accommodations and services a school can and cannot offer to be sure it is appropriate.

After the Diagnosis Has Been Made, What Then?

Depending on the nature of your child's learning disability and the level of understanding of and support for children with learning disabilities present in your community, you may want to consider the options available to you for your child's high school experience. In some cases, your local public high school will have the appropriate resources available to meet the needs of your child. In others, however, you may want to consider independent or parochial schools that may offer specialized services appropriate for your child. When choosing a high school for a child with learning disabilities, it is important to consider a variety of factors including the school's graduation requirements, the level of understanding and services for students with learning disabilities, and the likelihood of the child's success within the school environment.

Some students with learning disabilities or attention deficit disorders will not require any substantial accommodations in high school. A student with AD/HD, for example, may simply need to take an appropriate dosage of a prescribed medication on a designated schedule. While the medication may need to be administered at school and by school officials, such service does not require specialized training or significant resources to offer it. Students who require more significant accommodations and services such as the support of a learning specialist, special technology, or learning tools may have needs beyond the scope of the school. For students in a public school setting, the school system must find a way to meet these needs. Public school systems may centralize support services in designated schools or centers or they may choose to pay a student's tuition at an independent school that offers the necessary services. It is important that parents consult with middle school teachers, counselors, and administrators about what type of setting and what services are needed for their child in high school.

In addition to considering whether or not a high school has the appropriate services in place to meet your child's need, it is important to be aware of and understand the school's graduation requirements and how they may impact your child. In some cases, a school might be willing to waive a graduation requirement if there is substantial documentation to support such an accommodation. Some schools, however, may not be willing or able, in the case of public schools mandated by state graduation requirements, to do so. It is important for parents to investigate the graduation requirements of a particular high school before their child's enrollment. A child with a receptive language disorder, one that affects her ability to discern specific sounds, for example, may preclude this student from meeting a specific foreign language requirement or studying foreign language at all. A school that requires its students to complete a certain level of language study may not be the best choice for such a student.

Standardized Testing and the Student with Learning Disabilities

Fortunately or unfortunately, standardized testing is a fact of life in the world of college admissions. For the parents of students with learning disabilities, the prospect of standardized testing causes even more anxiety than it does for those students without this concern. In some cases, LD students don't typically test well on such standardized instruments as the tests required for college admission. The recognition of the importance of standardized testing in the admissions process understandably concerns parents of students who historically may not have tested well.

Fortunately, the College Board and ACT, the major testing bodies, offer accommodations to students with learning disabilities when the appropriate documentation and circumstances are in place. For this reason, it is essential for parents to properly and routinely document their child's learning disability so that when the time comes to begin the college search and the necessary tests, the appropriate accommodations can be granted. As noted above, key to the process of obtaining accommodations on the PSAT, SAT I and II, AP exams, and the ACT is documentation that is recent, generally within three years, includes the specific diagnosis, the accommodations needed, and what services are routinely provided in the school setting. While documentation specifying the exact learning disability and indicating a particular service or adjustment is essential, certain procedures must also be followed before accommodations will be granted for standardized tests. It is essential that parents make contact with the staff member at their child's school who is responsible for certifying and processing the requests for testing accommodations so that they meet all relevant deadlines and requirements.

Accommodations

There are a range of accommodations that are available to eligible students on standardized tests. They range from extended time to complete the test to different testing formats and administration guidelines. Students who qualify for extended time will be granted a certain percentage of extra time in which to take the test. Students who have visual processing disorders or a disability such as dyslexia may require a large-print test booklet, or answer sheet, or that the test be administered by a reader. Students with especially poor handwriting, which is the symptom of a documented learning disability, may be allowed to use a word processor for standardized tests. Regardless of what kind of learning disability your child has, it is important to investigate what kind of accommodations may be available and beneficial to her.

"Flagging" Test Scores

One of the biggest concerns parents of LD students have had recently with regard to standardized tests administered under nonstandard circumstances is that while the accommodations may be justified and may allow the student to achieve scores more reflective of his ability, they may be discounted by college admissions officers who know they were obtained under such conditions. Until October 2003, all test scores obtained under nonstandard administrations were reported to colleges with a "flag." Such scores were designated with an asterisk. While it is impossible to determine whether or not each set of scores was viewed with bias or not, after significant pressure by various special interest groups and specific legal decisions, the College Board determined it would no longer "flag" test scores received under nonstandard conditions. The good news for parents about this development is that colleges will no longer be informed of the nonstandard administration and, therefore, there should be no concern that the test scores will be discounted by admissions officers. The "bad" news is that the absence of flagging has prompted the College Board to be more vigilant in its evaluation of the requests for accommodations. In some cases, high school officials have been unable to secure accommodations for students who have previously received them or who have similar diagnoses to students who have been approved in the past. The current climate in the area of standardized testing necessitates vigilance and responsibility on the part of parents to be sure all procedures and testing requirements are met.

College Admission for Students with Learning Disabilities

One of the things it is important for parents of children with learning disabilities to remember is that while their college search must include consideration of the learning needs, it is merely one aspect of the college search, not the only feature. As is the case for all students and families beginning a college search, it is essential that students with learning disabilities assess their strengths, weaknesses, interests, and goals in addition to the specific accommodations and support services they may need. Before a meaningful college search can begin, families need to have a clear understanding of what type of services are needed.

As in middle and high school, there are varying levels of support and types of services available at the college level. Some colleges offer comprehensive learning support services, including a learning center staffed by trained learning specialists. Other colleges offer a much lower level of service but such circumstances may be appropriate for your child, depending upon her specific needs. There are several guides to colleges for students with learning disabilities. Two of the most prominent are *The K & W Guide to Colleges for Students with Learning Disabilities and ADD* and *Peterson's Guide to College Programs for LD Students*. Students and parents can also conduct on-line searches for colleges with LD support services at the various college search engines such as *www.collegeboard.com, www.petersons.com*, and *www.review.com*.

Comprehensive Programs

Colleges that offer comprehensive programs generally have a freestanding learning center, staffed by trained learning specialists. Students with learning disabilities will meet regularly with a specific learning specialist who will work with them individually, designing a plan for academic success. The learning specialist will monitor the services required and offered to each student, making sure that the student makes progress. While the student must take the initiative and be responsible for her own learning and schoolwork, there is significant support in place to ensure her success. Comprehensive programs may also offer remediation courses, a curricular option not generally available at schools that do not feature an extensive program of support for students with learning disabilities. At colleges that offer a comprehensive LD program within a traditional college environment and curriculum, there may be an additional fee structure, sometimes on a sliding scale based upon the services required for such services.

Specialized Curricula

There are also many colleges that offer a specialized curriculum to fully support the needs of LD students. These schools serve a primarily learning disabled student body. They may be two-year schools geared toward preparing students to move on to four-year programs without the same level of support. Schools offering a program designed to meet the particular needs of LD students are institutions such as Landmark College in Vermont and Curry College in Massachusetts.

"Moderate" Service

The next level of service is described as "moderate." At such schools, there is significant support available to students but not the intense monitoring or individualized attention that characterizes a comprehensive program. There is likely a Student Services Coordinator, who serves as an advocate for LD students, requesting extended time from professors on their behalf and procuring priority course registration to insure proper placement. There may also be a broad range of tutoring services available but there most likely will not be a learning specialist assigned to the student to serve as her specific advocate. Students who plan to attend a school with moderate services will need to have strong self-advocacy skills and be able to describe what it is she needs.

Uncoordinated Services

The lowest level of service is characterized by uncoordinated services available to all students. LD students, like any on campus, will need to seek out the support they need as no one will likely be monitoring their progress closely. Services available on these campuses may include a writing center and tutors but not the comprehensive, organized program and supervision available at colleges with greater support. Acquiring extended time on exams, a relatively easy-to-administer accommodation, is usually available even at schools with less significant support for LD students. The imperative factor for students to consider who attend colleges that offer this level of support is whether or not they can serve as their own advocate. Students who cannot clearly articulate their needs or pursue the services they need on their own may not find success in such an environment.

Self-Advocacy Skills

When determining which level of service is appropriate for a student, her self-advocacy skills must be considered. A student who has even significant learning disabilities may be served well by a college that offers services, not a comprehensive program, if the student is able to clearly identify her needs and seek the support she needs. Self-awareness is key to determining what is appropriate and beneficial in this process.

Transcript Evaluation

Another important consideration in the college search of an LD student is how any adjustments to high school graduation requirements or any variations of a typical high school course load might impact the evaluation of her transcript by admissions officers. For example, a student who has a waiver from a foreign language requirement in high school may find it difficult or impossible to gain admission to a college that has a strict policy requiring language study. Some states such as North Carolina have instituted policies at their publicly funded colleges and universities that restrict enrollment to students who have completed specific high school course requirements, including, for instance, two years of foreign language for admission. Acquiring such information through research and investigation and attending college guidance programs offered by your school or district will be essential to a successful college search.

Should the LD Be Disclosed?

When applying for admission to the colleges and universities you have selected, one consideration is whether or not to disclose the student's learning disability. By law, under the Americans with Disabilities Act, institutions are not allowed to ask whether or not a student has any type of disability, learning, physical, or otherwise. It is often, however, in the student's best interest to disclose this information as it helps the admissions office make the most valid and appropriate admission decision. It is in no one's interest for a student to be admitted to and attend a college that is not able to meet her individual needs. Such circumstances could be setting the student up for failure, something no college wants to do. Additionally, should a student be admitted to a particular college or university that is not aware of the disability at the time of admission, that institution is not required to provide the accommodations needed to allow for success. When considering whether or not to report the learning disability to colleges, parents should remember that most admissions officers value a student who is able to overcome difficulties and achieve even in light of obstacles. Students who meet with academic success in spite of learning disabilities have done just that and should be proud of themselves.

Although it may seem scary to parents as they begin to come to grips with their child's learning disability, foreseeing a challenging future that might be different than initially expected, a diagnosis of a learning disability does not preclude academic success or college attendance. It does, however, mean that parents have to educate themselves and be prepared to be strong and effective advocates for their child and her needs. Helping the child, when it is age-appropriate to do so, to understand her own learning needs, and become her own advocate will help insure future academic success as well.

QUESTIONS TO ASK

- What is my child's learning style?
- What services and accommodations does she need?
- Who is the school staff member responsible for working with students with learning disabilities?
- What is the school's philosophy regarding children with learning disabilities?
- What services and accommodations are available to students with learning disabilities?
- Will my child's access to courses be limited in any way based upon her learning profile?

A CHECKLIST FOR PARENTS OF CHILDREN WITH LEARNING DISABILITIES OR AD/HD

❏ Have your child tested for a learning disability when and if it is recommended by school personnel or your pediatrician.

❏ Can you accurately describe your child's learning disability? If not, work with the school counselor to understand clearly your child's learning profile.

❏ Become familiar with the services available to LD students within your child's school and community.

❏ Become familiar with local and state regulations related to LD students in order to be an effective advocate for your child.

❏ Understand what accommodations your child needs and what is required to obtain them.

❏ Be sure your child's psychoeducational evaluation and testing is current, comprehensive, and accurate.

Chapter 9

Covering College Costs

The Financial Aid Process and What You Can Do Now

A s you read article after article in the news media about the sky-rocketing cost of higher education, you might wonder if college is truly an option. And, if it is, is it one that is worthwhile? According to the National Center for Education Statistics (NCES), the cost of attending college, at either a public or private institution has more than doubled since 1980. The average total cost of attending a public four-year college has increased 2.4 times to $6,103 per year in the 2000–2001 academic year. This cost is up from $2,550, the average cost in 1980. Even more daunting, the average total cost of a private four-year college has almost tripled from 1980 when it was $5,594; the average total cost in 2000–2001 was $16,262.

While the cost of college may seem prohibitive and you may question the value of higher education to your child's future, study after study suggests that postsecondary study is worth its cost. Higher education affords students access to a broader range of career options and statistics show that the eventual earnings of college graduates is higher than that of individuals who do not complete bachelor's degrees—and, those who complete advanced degrees earn even more. The decision to attend college should be based on more than just earning potential, however. It should be about broadening one's perspective, finding one's personal code of ethics, and gaining a strong educational and cultural foundation upon which to build. But when a family considers that the cost of college attendance for one child can meet or exceed the cost of one's home, it is understandable that the potential economic return of the decision is an important consideration.

What Is the Economic Value of a College Education?

Although starting salaries can fluctuate with the economy over the course of one's working life, the economic return of a college degree, any college attendance for that matter, is significant and higher than without. In general, the higher the educational level attained, the higher the salary. The one exception is that those who earn professional degrees (Law, Veterinary, Medical, Chiropractic, Business), which typically require fewer years of study than doctoral (Ph.D.) programs, on average earn higher salaries than those who complete their doctorate. Below is a chart depicting average salaries by educational level as reported by the National Center for Education Statistics for the year 2000.

Gender	Some HS	HS Graduate	Some College	Associate Degree	Bachelor's Degree	Master's Degree	Prof. Degree	Doctorate
Male	$25,095	$34,303	$40,337	$41,952	$56,334	$68,322	$99,411	$80,250
Female	$17,919	$24,970	$28,697	$31,071	$40,415	$50,139	$58,957	$57,081

The difference in earnings for those who complete any college study versus those who complete only high school is an increase of $27,565, or 45 percent, for men and $17,736, or 42 percent, for women. The numbers are staggering and, therefore, worthy of a parent's full consideration.

Other factors certainly impact earnings potential, including a person's chosen career field and major course of study in college. There are many people who graduate from college who choose careers that may not result in earnings that meet the predicted average of those with college degrees. Additionally, there are those, obviously, who exceed the average earnings of their educational level by substantial amounts for a variety of reasons including their own initiative, creativity, and work ethic. As your child begins to discover areas of interest and skill, it may be interesting to you to know the average salaries of individuals who graduated with a particular major. Below is a chart that lists the average starting salaries by college major as reported by the National Association of Colleges and Employers (NACE) in its Summer 2003 Salary Survey.

Major	Average Starting Salary
Accounting	$40,546
Marketing/Marketing Management	$34,628
Business Administration/Management	$37,122
Economics/Finance	$40,084
Information Science and Systems	$39,787
Civil Engineering	$41,352
Computer Engineering	$51,720
Electrical/Electronic Engineering	$49,946
Mechanical Engineering	$48,441
English Language and Literature/Letters	$30,157
Criminal Justice and Corrections	$29,324
Psychology	$27,454
History	$32,108
Political Science/Government	$31,760
Elementary Teacher Education	$28,040
Secondary Education	$29,613
Biological/Life Sciences	$30,595
Sociology	$27,478

It is important to remember that money isn't everything and, while it may bring material comfort and convenience, it cannot provide personal fulfillment. That doesn't mean, however, that it hurts to be aware of the facts, especially because the initial investment is so large. Regardless of your reasons for providing the opportunity for your child to attend college, however, his matriculation will be valuable to him and to you.

An Overview of the Basics of Financial Aid

If you're reading this book, chances are you've decided that college is something you want your child's future to include. What you may not have figured out, however, is how to pay for such an investment. And, it is an investment—in his future, in his welfare, and in his personal fulfillment. For all of these reasons, attending college is a good investment, but it is one for which most of us must plan. Because the cost of a private college education for one child, let alone two or three, is likely to equal or exceed the price of a home, even those of significant means must be prepared to meet this expense. For most college students, however, even careful financial planning doesn't allow them to meet their educational expenses. According to NCES, 55.3 percent of all undergraduates, full- and part-time students, received some form of financial assistance in the 1999–2000 academic year.

When considering only those students enrolled in a college or university setting full time, the percentage of students receiving financial assistance has grown steadily over the past decade. Given the likelihood of continued increases in the cost of college, this growth will most likely continue. NCES reports that in the 1992–1993 academic year, 58.7 percent of students in all types of higher educational settings (including two-year and four-year, public and private, not-for-profit and for-profit schools) received some type of aid. That percentage grew in the 1995–1996 academic year to 68.4 percent and jumped again in 1999–2000 to 72.5 percent. Fortunately, there are many sources of financial assistance available to students and families; it just takes a little work and awareness to find them.

With Our Good Income, Can We Still Qualify for Financial Aid?

One of the most important things to remember when considering the likelihood of receiving financial aid is that the situation of each student or family is evaluated on an individual basis. Additionally, because the process is laden with forms and paperwork, sometimes extra explanation of individual circumstances may be needed. It is important, however, to recognize that, as in regard to myths surrounding the admissions process, there are legends about financial aid awards that are erroneous and misleading as well. Many have heard of the student, for example, who received an "athletic scholarship" to a Division III school. Such schools, by definition of their membership in the NCAA's Division III, cannot award financial aid based upon athletic talent; these tales, however, persist. When it comes time to begin considering the financial aid process, be sure to keep a level head and avoid the pitfalls of the rumor mill.

Because the application process for financial assistance can seem arduous and cumbersome, it may help to have some sense of whether or not you will qualify at all. Additionally, for those planning ahead, it is helpful to have an understanding of whether or not there is an income threshold for qualification and if so, where it is. According to NCES, there is a remarkably broad income range that will qualify families for some form of financial assistance. Keep in mind that the factors considered by financial aid officers are many and varied. Merely falling within a certain income range will not guarantee or preclude qualification for receiving financial assistance. Below is a chart compiled by NCES that reflects financial aid awards by family income level during the 1999–2000 academic year.

Income Range	Received Aid of Any Type	Grants	Loans	Work Study	Other
Less than $20,000	77.4%	75.0%	35.8%	12.2%	5.1%
$20,000–$39,999	67.6%	61.1%	38.8%	11.9%	6.6%
$40,000–$59,999	57.5%	42.7%	38.1%	9.9%	8.3%
$60,000–$79,999	53.8%	34.7%	36.6%	8.0%	9.4%
$80,000–$99,999	52.3%	33.2%	32.6%	5.5%	8.8%
$100,000 or more	44.4%	28.7%	24.4%	4.2%	8.3%

What Financial Aid Can We Qualify For?

In the world of college financial assistance, there are a number of different resources available to fund college attendance. The sources of this funding are varied. The federal government is the largest source of financial aid with, according to NCES statistics, 57.7 percent of the 72.5 percent of all full-time undergraduates who receive aid, receiving federal support. State governments, individual colleges and universities, private corporations, and nonprofit foundations are all also providers of financial aid. The criteria for receiving assistance vary and can be based upon the student's financial need, talents he possesses, personal characteristics, or familial ties.

When considering the cost of college attendance, one of the most important things for parents to understand is that if your family qualifies for financial assistance, the cost of the college or university your child attends may become less important. In other words, families should try to recover from the sticker shock of a college education so they may realize that if they qualify to receive financial aid, that qualification is based on a family contribution that remains static regardless of the cost of the college. As a result, it may cost a family the same amount for a child to attend an expensive private school as it does for that same child to attend a local public university. There are many factors that may make the local public university the better choice, but one of the main goals of federal and institutional financial aid programs is to insure equal access to higher educational opportunities to students from all income levels. So, as hard as it may be to believe, you may be able to consider some of the nation's most expensive schools if, in fact, they meet the other criteria you feel are best suited to your child's strengths, interests, and needs.

Types of Financial Aid

There are two basic types of financial aid available: need-based and merit-based. When considering college admission and financial aid, it is necessary to understand the difference between the two. The essential difference between need-based aid and merit-based aid is that one cannot qualify for need-based aid unless a true financial need exists as determined by the documentation provided by a family during the application process, while one can qualify for merit-based aid regardless of financial circumstances.

Need-Based Aid

Need-based aid is available in many forms. Utilizing many sources, federal, state, and institutional funds, colleges and universities provide a range of financing options to their students. From grants to college work study programs, students are able to meet their college costs. Some forms of aid are gifts to the student and family and are not required to be repaid, while others take the form of loans that, while often at a very low interest rate, must be repaid upon leaving college. Following is a listing of terms related to the financial aid process and their definitions.

Grants

Grants are gifts in aid given by colleges and universities to students who demonstrate financial need. Because grants do not need to be repaid, they are the most attractive financial aid component within a financial aid package. Grants are sometimes called scholarships. The term scholarship, however, refers to a gift in aid that is not based upon demonstrated financial need.

Loans

Arguably the least appealing factor within a financial aid package, loans are often a staple in making college affordable. Loans can be taken out by the student or his parents. Often loans obtained by parents carry a higher interest rate and may need to be repaid immediately upon disbursement. Loans obtained by students may be subsidized by the government and usually do not need to be repaid until the student leaves college and/or the interest payments can be deferred until such time.

College Work Study

This program, subsidized by the federal government, provides students with funding to meet their college costs through employment. Students secure positions on campus in settings ranging from an academic department office to the university gym. The pay they receive for their work is factored into their financial aid packages to defray personal costs such as books, meals, etc. Averaging usually less than 15 hours of work per week, students who participate in a work-study program do not risk poor grades or weaker than predicted academic performance. In many ways, students with some sort of activity that brings structure to their time, often perform better academically as they learn stronger time management skills.

Merit-Based Aid

Unlike need-based aid, merit-based awards are available to any student regardless of need. Another difference is that merit-based awards are almost always given in the form of grants, or in this case, scholarships. Such awards, as a result, rarely need to be repaid. The criteria for receiving a merit-based award vary. At some institutions, the criteria are solely academic. Based upon either their high school record, test scores, or some combination of the two, students qualify for a financial award. In some cases, the merit awards may be given on a sliding scale based upon the level of achievement, with stronger students receiving larger awards than those who are relatively weaker.

Merit-based awards can be given to recognize a variety of talents. Whether with some regard to a minimum academic standard or not, some merit-based awards are given on the basis of athletic, artistic, or other personal talent. What all merit-based awards have in common is that they recognize and reward a specific talent that the particular student possesses at a level much higher than the average applicant.

ROTC Scholarships

As there are college's devoted to preparing young men and women to serve their country in our nation's military, there is a substantial scholarship program designed to help students who choose not to attend a service academy meet the costs of college. There are ROTC, Reserve Officer Training Corps, and scholarships available for three branches of the military: Navy (NROTC), Army (AROTC), and Air Force (AFROTC). Competition for ROTC scholarships is keen and recipients may use their funding at a broad range of colleges and universities across the country. Recipients of an ROTC scholarship receive full tuition, room and board, and a generous stipend for books and living expenses. As those who attend one of the service academies, however, they must repay the country through active-duty military service. Students must also enroll in military science courses, maintain and participate in an often rigorous physical training routine, and generally serve some sort of summer military duty. Information about ROTC scholarships including how to apply and which colleges and universities sponsor them is available at:

1. Air Force ROTC—*www.afrotc.com*
2. Army ROTC—*www.armyrotc.com*
3. Navy ROTC—*http://www.nrotc.navy.mil/*

How Do We Qualify for Funding?

This question is much more easily answered when one is considering need-based financial aid. Because federal funds are often involved, the methodology for determining a family's need is explicit. In its most basic form, the formula used to determine if a student qualifies for need-based aid is the total cost of attendance minus the expected family contribution. If the result is greater than zero, the student demonstrates need. If the result is zero or less, the student will not qualify for aid.

What constitutes the expected family contribution is determined by what factors an institution considers in its awarding of aid. The sources of aid available to an institution also have a significant impact on how the family contribution is determined. If a college or university must rely only on federal and state forms of aid, then it must rely solely on the federal methodology when determining need. A college or university gains flexibility in providing financial aid when it possesses institutional funds, garnered either by a substantial endowment or tuition revenue, which are allocated for needy students. Such colleges use institutional methodology and may consider different factors when determining a family's financial need.

Two Forms to Determine Financial Aid

There are two forms commonly used by colleges and universities to determine financial need. These two forms are the FAFSA, the Free Application for Federal Student Aid, and the CSS/Financial Aid PROFILE, produced by the College Board. In addition to these forms, some colleges may also utilize an institutional form to determine how to disperse their own funds. The FAFSA and PROFILE are available in paper form at high schools, libraries, and other public venues as well as online. In both cases, the processing agencies prefer families to file the financial aid forms electronically. The FAFSA is available at *www.fafsa.ed.gov* and, as the name implies, is free to file. Families can register for the CSS/Financial Aid PROFILE at *www.collegeboard.com*; there is a $5 registration fee for those who apply for the PROFILE online, while there is a $7 fee when the registration is completed by phone. Additionally, there will be an $18 fee for each school to which the PROFILE results are sent.

Federal and Institutional Factors

The factors considered by federal and institutional methodology vary and an explanation is complicated. In general, the federal methodology allows for "losses that are permitted in the federal tax system" while the institutional methodology does not. Using institutional methodology, colleges can also take into account specific and significant expenses.

Institutional methodology, unlike the federal calculation, also considers home equity and the equity of other assets. The reason such considera-tion is made is because the home owner has consistent mortgage pay-ments, thereby allowing for financial planning, earns tax benefits as the result of any mortgage payments, and can draw on the equity in the asset to cover educational costs if necessary. Such consideration may seem unfair, especially in regions where home value is particularly high, but most would argue that the benefits of home ownership outweigh even this particular disadvantage.

Family Contribution

While the details of the methodology used to determine a family's expected contribution to cover college costs may be able to wait until the actual need to cover these costs is more imminent, one thing that is very beneficial to know early in your planning is that the parents' income and assets are viewed differently from the student's income and assets. Typically, the student is expected to contribute 50 percent of his income from the year prior to his enrollment in college to cover his educational costs. He is also expected to contribute 35 percent of all assets to his educational expenses. The income and assets of parents, however, are viewed differently because they typically have very differ-ent financial obligations than the student. The financial aid formulas recognize the needs of parents to provide housing, food, and other necessities for themselves, the student, and any other children. Additionally, because parents must plan for their own retirement, assets, in particular, are protected quite well under financial aid pro-grams. Parents, therefore, should consider the future ramifications of placing investments in their child's name. While there may be some tax benefit to investing in your child's name in the short run, the long-term financial disadvantage when it comes to covering college costs may be significant. Be sure to consult with a certified financial planner or tax consultant when planning to meet college costs.

The Components of a Need-Based Aid Package

Grants

Grants or gifts in aid can come from many sources including institutional funds. Many, however, are available because of federal and state funding sources. Some examples of grant programs are the Federal Pell Grant Program and Federal Supplemental Educational Opportunity Grant Program. These federal grants have strict income requirements for eligibility and are limited in their amounts. Individual institutions also award grants from their own financial resources.

Loans

There are many types of loans available to families to finance college costs. The "best" types of loans are those that are subsidized and, therefore, carry a lower interest rate. Like federal grants, federally subsidized loans are capped in the amounts available and have income requirements to qualify for loan eligibility. Some examples of loans are the Federal Stafford Loan Program, the Federal Direct Loan Program, the PLUS Loan Program, and the Federal Perkins Loan Program.

Work Study Programs

The Federal Work Study Program subsidizes the pay of college student employees. Colleges and universities across the country utilize federal funding to supplement the pay of its student employees, which allows students to work on campus in convenient jobs to augment their incidental budgets with the pay they receive for this work.

An Easy, Accurate Way to Determine Your Costs

While most of us, given the option, would love some sort of crystal ball that would provide us with information about where our child will be admitted to college, no such magic medium exists. Fortunately, and probably surprisingly, one does exist for financial aid. Families can go online, enter various financial data into a financial aid calculator, and, after waiting a few seconds, learn what it will cost them to send their child to college. These calculators are available on a number of sites including the ones listed below:

- *www.collegeboard.com*
- *www.finaid.org*
- *www.princetonreview.com*
- *www.usnews.com*
- *www.wiredscholar.com*

Parents should take advantage of this free, relatively easy exercise now and periodically as their child approaches college to be sure their financial planning remains sound.

Can Our Child's Strengths and Talents Help Us Pay for College?

Every parent knows the unique strengths and talents of their child. Some parents wonder if these talents and skills can be converted into funding for college. In some cases, the answer is yes. At colleges and universities across the country, people in enrollment planning and management have determined that offering financial rewards for achievement and talent in particular areas is the best way to attract high-caliber students to their campuses. These awards are institutional in nature and vary depending upon the individual priorities of the college or university that offers it.

Some colleges, seeking to improve the academic profile of its student body, will offer merit awards aimed at attracting students with especially strong academic records and high test scores. The program requirements and the amount of the awards will vary significantly from school to school. While the details of these programs will be very important at the time your child is ready to enroll in college, what is important to understand before you get to that point is that many of the nation's most prestigious colleges and universities don't offer merit-based awards. The reason they don't is because they are generally able to attract the brightest and most appealing applicants and would rather put their financial aid dollars toward aiding those who demonstrate financial need. It is also important to note that in order to be considered an appealing applicant for a merit-based award, a student will need to exceed the average characteristics of the applicant pool and even those of the average admitted student. Therefore, families hoping to secure a merit-based award given to students based upon their academic performance should consider colleges and universities where the child is at or near the top of the institution's applicant pool.

Criteria for Selection

When considering merit-based awards to recognize academic achievement, the criteria for selection can be quite clear and objective. Merit awards based on other talents, such as athletics, visual art, music, theater, etc., are much harder to define. When the time arrives for you and your child to consider whether or not he is a candidate for such an award, it is important to consult with your child's instructor or coach in the field of talent to determine if he is a viable candidate. No one, not even the admissions officers at the colleges in which you are interested, can predict whether or not your child will be recognized with such an award but they can help you meet the application requirements for the merit program. In cases of academic-based and talent-based (however, not athletic scholarships) merit award programs, there may be an extra application requirement. Such a supplemental form may include additional essays and even campus visits and interviews. Be sure you understand any special submission and format requirements for the program; missing out on a merit opportunity for a procedural mistake would be especially frustrating.

Finding Merit-Based Awards

The Internet has become a staple in finding everything from a local pizza delivery service to a 30-year fixed mortgage. It's no wonder then that the

Internet is a terrific resource for locating merit-based awards. There are a number of web sites that offer information about scholarships and will even sort through all of the available options for which your child is qualified. Some will even send you an electronic reminder when a scholarship application is due and notify you when a new program for which your child is a candidate is found.

One thing to keep in mind is that because the scholarship awards can be significant, the process of finding and applying for them can be time-consuming. It pays, therefore, to begin searching for and applying for these awards early in your child's senior year of high school. Some web sites that can be helpful are:

- *www.college-scholarships.com*
- *www.collegeboard.com*
- *www.collegenet.com*
- *www.collegeview.com*
- *www.embark.com*
- *www.fastweb.com*
- *www.finaid.org*
- *www.wiredscholar.com*

Financing College Costs—What You Can Do Now

Regardless of the age of your children, there are things you can do now to offset some or all of the costs of their college education. Enlisting the aid of a certified financial planner is probably the best way for a parent to successfully secure the funding for higher education. There are many ways to finance college; some methods are designed specifically to pay for educational costs, while others are simply good means for planning financially for any future goals. In consultation with a financial planner, families must determine which method is best for them based upon their own distinct circumstances. What should be understood is that many educational savings tools require the funds to be utilized for costs associated with education, and students and families may incur significant penalties if they are not utilized for these costs.

There are many types of investment tools available for saving for the cost of college. Some of these programs are sponsored by individual states; others are managed by the nation's premier financial institutions. Each state and the District of Columbia have started either prepaid tuition plans for qualified state tuition savings plans, making saving for college manageable no matter where in the country one lives. Whatever your needs and situation, there is likely a plan that can help you save. Below are some of the common educational savings plans.

529 Plans

Currently one of the most popular means of saving for college, 529 plans offer families a great way to boost college savings. Plan earnings and withdrawals are exempt from federal taxes if they are used for educational purposes and there are generous contribution caps making it possible to make significant savings.

Prepaid Tuition Plans

Many states offer prepaid tuition plans. There are two types of prepaid plans. For those who can, families pay for all four years in advance to avoid any inflationary costs. The more common prepaid plan allows families to spread the costs of college over a longer period of time, shrinking the size of each payment.

Qualified State Tuition Savings Programs

These programs are also often referred to as state-sponsored 529 plans. Such investment programs are tax-deferred and when the funds are withdrawn, they are taxed at the usually lower child's rate. 529 plans have neither income level or contribution amount limits, making them somewhat more popular than Coverdell accounts.

Coverdell Education Savings Account

This program allows almost anyone from family members to friends to set up an educational savings account in the name of a student. Contributions of up to $2,000 can be made annually and while they are not tax deductible during the year they are made, the earnings of the account will not be taxed until they are withdrawn. It is important to note that there are income restrictions on Coverdell contributions.

Saving Money for College Expenses Without Even Trying

How often do we all wish we could have something for nothing, or close to nothing? Believe it or not, in the most unlikely of areas—paying for college—it is possible to get something for very little effort and no cost to you. Started in 2001, Upromise is probably the easiest way to save for college expenses. The program has solicited the sponsorship of businesses, both national and local, that have pledged to contribute a percentage of each purchase of their product or service by a Upromise member to the individual's account. The proceeds of this account can then be transferred to a 529 plan for future college expenses. There is no cost to the participant, who must simply register his credit, debit, or check cards with Upromise. Upromise members may also sign up for the organization's credit card, which increases their savings opportunities as a percentage of all purchases made with it are contributed to their account. From the purchase of gas to office supplies, Upromise members can accumulate big savings, especially if they start early.

The Student's Role in the Process

While most can agree that it is the parents' responsibility to provide for their children, that doesn't mean our children should take higher education, or other privileges for that matter, for granted. One of the greatest learning experiences we can afford our children as we begin to plan for their education is helping them understand what it will cost. Without causing undue stress on younger children, it may be helpful for them to know that each month you are putting money into an account for their college costs. Certainly, regardless of what the goal is, helping children to understand the need for financial planning and savings will be helpful to them well beyond their college years. As parents, seizing this opportunity is a way to benefit not only your child in the long run, but help them understand and appreciate the sacrifices, large or small, that you are making to ensure their education. Such knowledge will illustrate clearly to your child the confidence you have in them, their abilities, and their future. What a wonderful message to send!

QUESTIONS TO ASK

- Are we doing what we can to plan for our child's education now?
- Which savings options are best for us, given our income, assets, and personal situation?
- What are the options available for college savings in our home state?

A CHECKLIST FOR SOUND FINANCIAL PLANNING

❑ Schedule meeting with certified financial planner to determine best means to meet college costs.

❑ Determine what sacrifices may need to be made now to ensure future access to college.

❑ Log on to an online family contribution calculator to check family's potential for receiving financial aid.

❑ Investigate *www.Upromise.com* and consider registering with this online service.

Chapter 10

After College—What Comes Next?

I f your child is in the early grades of middle school, or even the later ones, for that matter, the prospects of life after college probably seem pretty far removed. With the intense focus today on which college a child attends, sometimes it's hard to remember that it is what college prepares one for that is further reaching and, therefore, more important in the full overview of someone's life. Understanding the options for after college and how to reach each of them is important.

Options

Employment

There are many options for life after college, including the obvious, employment. So often we meet people who may have "fallen into" their field of work—or we may be those people ourselves—and while most are happy with where they have landed, we all know those who wish they had realized the options available to them in order to have exerted more choice in the matter. Parents can help their children understand what paths lie ahead in order to help them make good and appropriate choices when the time comes, because, in addition to entering the work force immediately after college, there are many types of graduate programs they can pursue as well as volunteer programs in which they can participate. All options have merit and all have intrinsic satisfaction. Knowing which is right, though, can be especially difficult and frustrating for a young person.

For high school seniors (and sometimes their parents), the most dreaded, and yet most asked, questions are "What will you be doing next year?" or "Where are you going to college?" As a student nears her last year of college, the questions start again, only this time, with the options so vast, they can produce even more anxiety and uncertainty. While figuring out where one wants to spend four years of college is certainly a big task, determining how to spend the next 30 or 40 years is downright intimidating. Fortunately, there are support systems in place at most colleges to help a student narrow her interests and focus on a more manageable number of postcollege plans.

Graduate Study

Some students will decide that their career goals require graduate-level study. Others will want to continue their education simply because they are driven by an intense desire to further their depth of understanding in a field or seek an advanced degree. Sometimes external factors such as the job market and economy make remaining in school a more appealing option. History has shown that when the economy is strong and jobs are plentiful, graduate school applications drop. The converse is true as well, so that when the economy is weak, applicants to graduate programs increase, probably because students hope to wait out the tight job market while gaining education and skills that will serve them well once it recovers. Whatever the reason, graduate school is generally a very good option. Study after study supports the notion that while college attendance of any duration generally leads to increased earning potential, graduate-level study boosts salary possibilities even more, not to mention the fact that the range and level of positions one is qualified for increased as well with advanced study.

Volunteer and Community Service

In addition to the traditional postcollege options of working and continued education, college graduates today have some impressive volunteer or community service options available to them as well. Programs such as AmeriCorps and Teach for America allow graduates to serve their country or a local community, putting to use their skills, talents, and education. Like the Peace Corps, which has sent generous-minded, able people to the far reaches of the world for decades, more recently conceived programs such as AmeriCorps and Teach for America keep equally impressive young men and women here in our own country, working to better the lives of others. Whether one has interest in traveling abroad or staying within our borders, programs designed to improve conditions and services in needy communities can offer young people the opportunity to develop valuable, transferable skills and experiences, the memories of which, can last a lifetime.

For more information about these remarkable service-work programs, visit their web sites at:

1. AmeriCorps—*www.americorps.org*
2. The Peace Corps—*www.peacecorps.gov*
3. Teach for America—*www.teachforamerica.org*

How to Start

Sometimes the hardest part of making a decision is getting started. With so many options available and the stakes seemingly so high, it can be very difficult to figure out in which direction one wants to go. Often, there are resources available through colleges and even high schools. In high school, the guidance office may have interest inventory instruments or have site licenses for web sites that help a student determine her interest profile; your middle school may also even have some sort of similar resource available. As a parent, it may be helpful to review the programs and services available at your middle and high school in order to take full advantage of helpful tools.

At the high school or middle school level, the extent of career guidance services will depend largely on the student population and the community served by the school. In areas where very few students continue to college or where other more pressing issues related to encouraging students to continue high school long enough to earn a diploma take precedence, comprehensive career or college guidance may be a lower priority. Schools, though, that serve a primarily college-bound population or that may be located in an area that has a substantial job market that requires skilled employees may offer career education and planning services. In many cases, however, it is at the college level that students will first encounter broad and substantial career-planning programs.

Interest Assessment Tools

Many adults have taken the Myers-Briggs Interest Inventory at some point in their life or read an edition of *What Color Is My Parachute?* in an effort to find some direction for their own career. Today, though, interest assessment tools are available to a much wider audience, either through high school guidance offices, college career centers, or via online surveys. Even web sites devoted primarily to the college search may also include abbreviated interest inventory instruments. Today's students are so acclimated to using their computers for everything from academic research to "talking" with their friends through instant messaging, taking an online quiz is almost second nature and easily accomplished. The College Board's web site, *www.collegeboard.com*, offers a short and easy way to use interest assessment, which then allows students to investigate careers that may be appropriate and the majors that will prepare students to pursue them. This site is free to students but there are others that may offer a more extensive instrument for a fee. Families, if they feel it is warranted, may also choose to see a psychologist trained to administer the Myers-Briggs Interest Inventory or a career counselor to help define potential areas of interest. Your school's guidance office or student services office may be able to provide referrals to career counseling professionals.

Graduate School Options

Once your child has determined what her goals are, if they include graduate study, it is helpful to understand the basic requirements for admission for some of the most popular types of schools.

GRE

Students who wish to pursue an advanced degree in a specific academic discipline such as English, history, or biology will find they need to take the graduate school version of the SAT, otherwise known as the GRE or Graduate Record Examination. This test has three components including sections covering verbal, quantitative, and analytical writing skills. As is the case in college admission, a student's performance on the GRE can significantly impact the list of schools to which a student has access, but as in undergraduate admission, it is merely one of the components considered. Information about the GRE can be obtained by visiting *www.gre.org.*

Medical School

As you know, if your child hopes to become a physician, she has many years of coursework and practical training ahead of her. Admission to medical school is traditionally extremely competitive. Students must compile an exceptional academic record within a rigorous course of undergraduate study and score well on the Medical College Admissions Test (MCAT). College coursework, including one year each in English, biology, chemistry, organic chemistry, physics, and calculus or statistics, is the minimum preparation recommended. While there was a time when virtually every student who wished to go to medical school chose to major in biology, now students study history, English, even business in preparation for a career in medicine. Students have found that even with a different major focus they are still able to get the preparation needed for medical school as long as they complete the basic course of study. Medical schools find students of any background appealing as long as they possess the foundation needed for advanced study. Standardized test scores, the MCATs, are integral to the medical school admissions process. While many applicants to college will choose not to pursue professional test preparation for the SAT I or ACT, virtually all medical school hopefuls will. MCAT preparation is not a luxury; in many cases it is a necessity. Students who are interested in investigating the requirements for medical school, may find a visit to the web site of the Association of American Medical Colleges at *www.aamc.org* helpful.

One of the ways a college woos particularly able students interested in a career in medicine is by touting an especially high medical school placement record. Some colleges manipulate this statistic by limiting those students who are eligible to apply to medical school, weeding out those who may not succeed in the process by pulling their support, refusing to endorse the student's application with a letter of recommendation. When investigating colleges, therefore, if your child is interested in studying medicine, it is important to ask not only what the acceptance rate is to medical school but whether or not the college limits the number it will endorse in the application process.

Law School

Law school is another popular destination for graduate study. Like medical school, there is a specific standardized test requirement for admission and generally, admission is competitive. While acceptance rates to law school in general may be somewhat higher than those for medical school, competition for admission to the nation's top programs is quite keen. Top grades and an impressive LSAT (Law School Admission Test) score are often prerequisites for admission to the nation's most prestigious law schools. As is the case with the MCAT, most students serious about entering law school enroll in professional test preparation programs to prepare for the LSAT. The LSAT score can often determine whether or not a student will gain admission to one of the nation's most prestigious law schools. Information about the LSAT can be viewed at the Law School Admission Council web site at *www.lsac.org.*

History and political science majors remain popular choices for those who hope to attend law school but other courses of study that develop strong critical thinking, analytical, and communication skills such as economics, English, even theater have become appealing options as well. The ability to express oneself clearly and persuasively is particularly beneficial to a law student and an attorney. Many are able to memorize legal tenets and case histories, but the ability to communicate and influence others in combination with a sound legal foundation make for a very effective attorney.

Business Schools

Although students who hope to pursue an MBA may find it beneficial, even necessary, to work for a few years before entering a graduate program, their collegiate performance and Graduate Management Admission Test (GMAT) scores are critical to admission. The GMAT includes three sections: the Analytical Writing Assessment, the Quantitative section, and the Verbal section. Because business schools value practical experience and training, work experience can be a valuable component in a prospective student's application. Prior work experience is not the only consideration. As is the case with other professional schools, however, the nation's top programs require strong scores on the GMAT in addition to solid coursework. Information about the GMAT and applying to business schools can be found at the Graduate Management Admission Council's web site at *www.mba.com.*

Regardless of what your child hopes to study in graduate school, seeking the assistance of the appropriate college staff in determining the best course of study and preparing for the necessary standardized test will be beneficial when the time comes to apply.

College Career Planning and Placement Centers

Whether your child decides to pursue a graduate degree or enter the workforce, a career planning and placement center is a valuable resource to help her reach her goals. Most, if not all, colleges and universities will have career planning and placement centers. While many students will not venture into such an office until the end of their junior year or later, most career centers offer programs that are geared toward younger students and can provide valuable information for those who are trying to figure out what they want and where they want to go. Career centers offer a broad range of services, determining what is available at the colleges your child might want to attend and who can take advantage of the offerings can be useful to include in a comprehensive college search.

In today's society we are focused often on outcomes. We want to know what our investment will get us. Families investigating colleges and universities are no different. When choosing a college, families are making a substantial investment of time and money; considering all of the potential perks and returns of enrollment at one school over another has become an important factor in many college searches. As you begin to investigate college options and visit campuses, a phone call to the career center or perhaps a stop there during your tour may prove valuable.

When visiting a career center, one of the first things to ask is whether or not the career-planning services are available to all students regardless of major or year of graduation. Most career centers welcome younger students who are interested in learning about themselves, their likes and dislikes, and their strengths, and using this information to develop a comprehensive and individualized educational and career plan. To meet the needs of students of all ages, career centers offer counseling services by trained career counselors and specialists. They may offer interest inventories or other assessment tools administered by a psychologist or counselor or via an online tool or counseling software. If administered correctly and completed properly, an interest inventory can be a powerful tool in helping a student determine her goals and how to reach them.

Job-Seeking Programs

While many students will take advantage of career counseling programs, unfortunately, many skip this step, jumping right into the more visible and seemingly more practical job-seeking programs often sponsored by career centers. Because such programs tend to be very visible and high-profile events, and because, frankly, it is a more obvious service to seek, it is understandable that students who may not know that something like career counseling exists may move right past the process of deciding what they want to do to find a job. Often, students who skip the career counseling step end up in a career field that is perfectly well suited to their needs, interests, and life goals. Sometimes, though, they end up in a job that is neither satisfying nor particularly well suited to their strengths and abilities. Because of the amount of time most of us spend working in our lives, it seems that taking the time to avail oneself of the generally free services of a college's career planning office makes a lot of sense. Guiding your child in this direction once she enters college will not only help her make better informed choices about her future but will allow her to take full advantage of the services offered by the college she attends, which, quite frankly, you are paying for.

Placement Services

Whether a student takes advantage of the career counseling programs offered by her college or not, most seek out the placement services they sponsor. Most college career centers offer résumé workshops, interview technique sessions, and on-campus recruiting programs. Career counselors or recruitment managers will work with students to help them fine-tune their interviewing skills and write and rewrite their résumés. These events tend to be the high-profile efforts of campus career centers because they prepare students for the job market and provide direct access to those who can offer employment. Students can see the correlation between participating in these types of programs and actually landing a job, making them a priority for any undergraduate.

One of the key responsibilities of a college career center is developing and maintaining relationships with employers. In a weak economy when jobs are at a premium and more experienced workers may be in the job market as companies downsize and reorganize, the ability of a college to draw corporate recruiters to campus is important. Many colleges and universities, even those with which you may not be as familiar, are hiring grounds for some of the most prominent and financially secure companies in the country and even the world. As you investigate college options for your child, you might find it helpful to speak with a career center representative and ask about the employers who routinely visit the campus and actually hire its graduates.

Beyond the Job Market

Although the thing most students know the career center for is the assistance it provides to those searching for a full-time, postgraduation position, it can also offer valuable support for those looking for a summer job or internship. As in other arenas, the college's alumni can play a key role in the school's efforts to help students find employment. Alumni can provide the framework for an instant network, and current students and recent graduates should tap into this powerful resource. Often, a member of the career center staff coordinates alumni programs that provide summer jobs, internships, and even full-time job opportunities for current students and recent graduates. Tapping into this network affords students tremendous access to interesting and meaningful work experiences.

Some college career centers may also be responsible for helping students apply to graduate programs. In many cases, academic departments or academic deans may also work closely with students who want to pursue a graduate degree. A student's academic advisor, typically someone in the department in which she is majoring, is the guiding force in her graduate school search and application process. For students interested in pursuing professional degrees such as an MBA or a law degree, the campus career center or a preprofessional advisory committee is likely the best source of information about graduate programs. They will guide a student toward the options available to her and provide the school's formal endorsement or recommendation to the programs to which she chooses to apply. In the case of medical school, an academic dean's office or a premed advisory committee may be charged with providing guidance and support for prospective applicants. Regardless who provides the information about graduate study, if your child hopes to pursue an advanced degree you should encourage her to seek out guidance early in her college career from those best suited to help her.

Helpful Opportunities for Undergrads

Any time someone can preview a potential career choice or other major life choice without actually having to make a commitment to it, it is a valuable opportunity. Internships and Co-op programs offered at the undergraduate level are just that. These types of practicum experiences allow students to gain hands-on experience in a particular field of interest during a defined period of time without a significant commitment. As is the case when people attend an open house in a neighborhood they've admired at a house they've coveted only to find an odd layout and hideous wallpaper, it is better to find out they don't like the place after a short visit as opposed to after the closing, so is it helpful to find out that a particular career field or job site is not appropriate after a short period of time and before investing significant educational resources.

Internships

Summer or academic year internships allow students to preview a proposed career field and to gain valuable workplace experience at the same time. Even if a student who interns in a law firm and decides that the legal field is completely unappealing to her is able to learn important lessons about workplace etiquette and employer expectations that will serve her well when she does find the career for her. A college's career planning and placement center is the best place to begin a search for an internship. Alumni and even parents of graduates and current students are valuable resources if a child has to pursue an internship on her own. Even the process of finding an internship and beginning to develop networking skills is valuable in and of itself.

Some colleges and universities offer academic programs that require an internship component in order to graduate. Such programs are generally called Co-op programs, referring to the cooperative nature of the offering. Schools such as Northeastern University in Massachusetts and Drexel University in Pennsylvania are leaders in the field of cooperative education and offer programs in a broad range of areas. Co-op programs, while appealing to many students, might be particularly appropriate for students who may find more success in hands-on settings as opposed to more traditional classroom situations. In some cases Co-op programs may take longer to complete than those that are not. Generally, however, if a student progresses at a normal pace, a Co-op degree should be completed within five years. Sometimes the structure of a Co-op program alternates traditional semesters that include only on-campus coursework with internship semesters that will not include classes. In other situations, the student will complete traditional on-campus semesters followed by Co-op programs during the summer. Regardless of the format, one of the drawbacks a student might see to a Co-op program is that it may extend beyond the typical four years required to complete an undergraduate degree or might necessitate year-round school or work commitments. While it is easy to understand why a student would see this circumstance as negative, it can be an especially rewarding option, for Co-op Programs and internships alike can be especially valuable in securing a full-time position in a student's chosen career field. Whether or not a specific Co-op position actually leads to a position with the host organization, a student can make valuable personal contacts and, at a bare minimum, gains professional experience to include on a résumé. For those recent graduates who face the timeless dilemma of needing a job but not being able to find one because they lack experience, the addition of a Co-op or internship experience to a résumé while looking for a first job is priceless.

Why Make Career Choices Before College?

We all know that the more interested we are in something or the better we can visualize the end result, the more likely we are to persist to our goal. If we can visualize ourselves as we reach our goal, our motivation level increases and we are more willing to accept the things we must do but may not like. Children, probably even more than adults, have difficulty delaying gratification so anything we can do as parents to help them understand that their goals make hard work and waiting worthwhile will help them to do their best and keep working until they achieve what they want.

Also important to success when meeting long-term goals is knowing what steps need to be completed in order to achieve them. Being able to check off the required tasks as they are completed is a powerful motivational tool as we are able to see what we have accomplished and how it relates to our overall goal. Understanding that it takes lots of little steps to reach our desired outcome also helps make it seem more realistic and less overwhelming. For a teenager who hopes to become a doctor, understanding the many steps ahead of her before she reaches that goal allows her to first make a good decision about whether the course is for her, then helps her manage them in order to stay focused and motivated. As anyone who has reached a long-term goal knows, getting closer to it and checking off the smaller tasks on the way can be very exciting as well.

Parents should not, however, read this and log on to an interest inventory site for their sixth grader. Even much older teens who appear very focused and consistent in their expressed goals will likely change their mind. Studies regarding college majors indicate that 50 percent or more of college students will change their intended major at least once. Admissions officers often joke that the most popular major on their campuses is "undecided." So don't rush your child but do support her efforts to investigate and pursue interests. That obsession with Legos or Hot Wheels as a child may lead to an interest in architecture or automotive engineering, but no one will know if she is not encouraged to try related school courses or extracurricular activities.

At the foundation of our job as parents is taking care of our child, preserving her well-being. While that job can be difficult even when they are young, it can become even more so as they grow and leave our care. At the root of all the parental anxiety that has become commonplace in today's college search is most likely the parents' need to insure that their child will be successful and able to care for herself. It is understandable, therefore, that parents want to know with certainty that their child knows what she wants to do and that the choice she has made is a good one. As hard as it may be not to take over and exert our own influence on our children's college and career path, parents must trust that they have instilled values and skills in them that will allow them to make their own best choices.

QUESTIONS TO ASK

- What career guidance tools and resources are available at my child's middle and high school?
- What does my child like to do in her free time?
- What academic subject is my child's favorite and in which is she most skilled?
- Is my child well or better suited to a more hands-on or practical academic program?

A Checklist for Career Planning

❏ Introduce child to career fields through "Take Your Child to Work"-type programs and by discussing careers with friends and relatives.

❏ As your child approaches college age, research various career fields and employment outlooks. Offer insight to your child if she expresses an interest in fields that are relatively weaker or stronger at that point in time.

❏ Support your child's interests by encouraging her involvement in after-school activities and other extracurricular programs.

Glossary of Terms

ACCEPTANCE RATE: The percentage of students accepted from the total applicant pool. The lower the acceptance rate, the more competitive admission is to the college or university. Generally, the lower the acceptance rate is, the higher a student's academic credentials must be to gain admission.

ACT: The ACT is one of two standardized tests commonly required for college admission. The ACT was once more commonly recognized and accepted in the western and midwestern portions of the United States, but in recent years it has become much more well known and more widely used throughout the country. The test includes four subsections (English, reading, math, and science) and is scored on a scale of 1–36.

ADVANCED PLACEMENT (AP) COURSES AND EXAMS: The Advanced Placement program is sponsored by the College Board and includes rigorous courses in a variety of fields. The curriculum for each course is prescribed by the College Board and culminates in a national exam administered on the same date at the same time at each participating school. The exams are scored on a scale of 1–5. Most colleges and universities participate in the College Board's AP program and will offer college credit for designated scores on AP exams.

APPLICANT POOL: The total number of students who apply in any given year to a specific college or university. Generally, the term "applicant pool" refers to first-year candidates for admission.

CANDIDATE'S REPLY DATE (Deposit Date): The Candidate's Reply Date is May 1st of each year and is the date by which students must respond to a school's offer of admission. Students must indicate to each college that offered them admission whether or not they will attend. Students must respond to the one school, and it is imperative that students reply positively to only one college, that they plan to enroll; generally, students must submit an enrollment deposit to secure their place in the class. The Candidate's Reply Date is a firm deadline and must be strictly adhered to.

CEEB CODE: The College Entrance Examination Board (CEEB) Code is the number assigned by the College Board to identify individual high schools and colleges. This code is used often in the college search process to apply for financial aid and register for all standardized tests including the ACT.

THE COLLEGE BOARD: The College Board is a nonprofit membership association. The membership includes both high school and college/university representatives. The College Board administers the SAT, PSAT, and AP program in addition to other educational efforts.

COLLEGE WORK STUDY: A component of need-based financial aid packages, the College Work Study program is a federally subsidized program that allows students to work on campus to supplement their income and meet the expenses of college. The student's salary is paid by the college and subsidized by a grant from the federal government.

CO-OP PROGRAMS: Co-op Programs are specialized programs offered by a relatively small number of colleges and universities that allow students to gain practical, hands-on experience in a professional work environment. Unlike an internship, a Co-op experience is a formal part of the academic curriculum and usually carries academic credit that will satisfy graduation requirements. An added bonus is that some Co-op positions are paid. One potential disadvantage of formal Co-op programs is they may lengthen the time needed to earn a bachelor's degree, as the Co-op experience does not always carry the same academic credit as traditional coursework.

CSS PROFILE: The College Scholarship Service (CSS), a division of the College Board, produces the CSS PROFILE. The PROFILE is required by many colleges and universities, often private institutions, to determine a student's eligibility for financial assistance. Students must first register to receive the PROFILE. Upon registration, the form will be sent to the student.

DEFERRED: Deferred is a status used by admissions staffs to postpone a final decision on an application. For example, students who apply for Early Decision or Early Action admission may be deferred as opposed to admitted or denied when the admissions staff would like to see more information, such as subsequent grades or test scores, before rendering a final decision.

DEFERRED ADMISSION: Occasionally, students will determine that they are unable to attend college for the semester to which they have been admitted. In this circumstance, the student may request a "deferral." The student will need to provide information about what he will be doing during the time prior to enrollment and the college or university will determine whether or not it can "hold" a space for him for the following semester or year. Generally, the student will be required to submit an enrollment deposit and sign an enrollment agreement in order to be granted a deferral. Should the student not enroll at the college or university, he will likely lose the enrollment deposit.

EARLY ACTION: Early Action is an admissions program offered by a relatively small number of colleges and universities, which allows students to apply for admission by a specific date then receive an admissions decision within a few weeks but without any obligation to enroll if admitted.

EARLY ADMISSION: Early Admission is an admissions program offered by some colleges that allows a student to enroll after his junior year. Under these circumstances, a student may not complete high school graduation requirements before enrolling in college. Students who require need-based financial aid will need a high school diploma to qualify for federal funding and should consider earning a General Equivalency Diploma, or GED, in place of their school's diploma. Generally, only particularly strong and mature students should consider this option.

EARLY DECISION: Early Decision is an admission program sponsored by relatively few colleges and universities under which students apply for admission by a designated date, normally in the fall, in order to receive an admissions decision within a few weeks. If admitted under an early decision agreement, students are obligated to enroll at that school.

EDUCATIONAL TESTING SERVICE (ETS): A division of the College Board that is responsible for the design of the SAT and other standardized tests it administers.

FAFSA: The FAFSA is the Free Application for Federal Student Aid. As the name implies, the form is free to file and determines a student's eligibility for federal financial assistance. Schools that require the FAFSA to determine eligibility for financial aid may also require the CSS PROFILE.

GRADUATION RATE: The graduation rate is the percentage of students who complete a college or university's graduation requirements within four or five years. A school's graduation rate is often a factor considered when families evaluate whether or not a particular college is an appropriate match for their child. A high graduation rate tends to imply that the college or university is successful in supporting students in their education.

GRANTS: Typically a component in need-based financial aid packages, grants are funds awarded to a student to help him meet the costs of college attendance. Grants do not need to be repaid and, therefore, may be referred to as scholarships. Grants, however, unlike scholarships, are based solely on a student's financial need status, not on any particular talent.

INTERNATIONAL BACCALAUREATE (IB) PROGRAM: The International Baccalaureate or IB Program is sponsored by the International Baccalaureate Organization and is offered in schools in the United States as well as other countries. It is a particularly rigorous course of study. Students at schools that offer the IB program can elect to take individual IB courses or complete the requirements of the full IB diploma. There are two levels of courses: higher level and subsidiary level. There is a year-end exam for each course that students may elect to take. Students who earn specific scores on the exams may earn college-level credit similar to those who do well on AP exams.

INTERNSHIPS: Internships have been an increasingly popular option for students on today's college campuses. Internships can provide valuable hands-on experience and networking opportunities, allowing students to test potential career interests.

LOANS: Arguably the least appealing component of a financial aid package, loans are one option a family may choose in order to meet the costs of attending college. Loans must be repaid to the lending institution. Loans can be subsidized, thereby lowering the interest rate or perhaps deferring the start of repayment. Generally, subsidized loans are available to students who demonstrate financial need. Unsubsidized loans are also available to students and families. These loans, while not supported by the school or government, are still generally fairly low interest.

MERIT-BASED FINANCIAL AID/SCHOLARSHIPS: Colleges and universities may recognize the academic or personal talents of specific students with monetary awards. These awards are forms of merit-based financial aid or scholarships. Not all colleges and universities offer merit-based financial aid. Generally, to be a competitive candidate for such an award, a student must exceed the average credentials of other applicants by a significant margin.

NATIONAL COLLEGIATE ATHLETIC ASSOCIATION (NCAA): The NCAA is the governing body of collegiate athletics. The NCAA provides recruitment guidelines and determines the academic standards students must meet to participate in collegiate athletics. The NCAA also monitors the conduct of collegiate athletic departments and officials.

NATIONAL MERIT SCHOLARSHIP PROGRAM: The National Merit Scholarship Program is a scholarship competition sponsored by a private corporation that uses the results of the PSAT to identify talented students to participate in the National Merit Scholarship competition. Only eleventh-graders who take the PSAT are eligible for participation in this program. This scholarship program is prestigious with ultimately only about $1^1/_2$ percent of those who take the PSAT earning distinction as a National Merit Scholar. The National Merit Scholarship Corporation also recognizes African-American students through the National Achievement Program and Hispanic students through the National Hispanic Recognition Program.

NEED-BLIND ADMISSION: Schools that are "need-blind" do not consider a student's ability to cover the cost of college expenses when making an admissions decision. Regardless of their financial status, students will be admitted if they are qualified and competitive for admission.

NEED-SENSITIVE ADMISSION: Colleges that practice a need-sensitive admissions process take into account a student's financial status. A student with significant financial need may be denied admission, while another with less or no financial need will be accepted even if he is a weaker applicant.

OPEN ADMISSION: Schools with open admission policies will admit any applicant regardless of academic credentials and preparation. The admission cycle is often open-ended allowing students to apply up to the start of classes.

PLAN: The PLAN is the practice ACT, which is administered to high school sophomores. It includes four subsections (English, reading, science, and math) and is scored on a 1–32 scale, similar to the ACT.

PSAT: The Preliminary Scholastic Assessment Test is the practice SAT I. Many high schools across the country administer the PSAT to tenth- and eleventh-graders.

REGULAR DECISION: A vast majority of college applicants apply under Regular Decision admissions programs. Such programs require students to apply by a specified deadline and all students will be notified of their admissions decision at the same time. Admitted students are under no obligation to enroll.

ROLLING ADMISSIONS: Schools that offer a rolling admission program allow students to apply for admission throughout a designated period of time and will notify students of their admissions decision once all required credentials are received and final decisions are made. Decisions, therefore, are made and released on a continuous or "rolling" basis.

SAT I: The SAT I is the primary standardized test required for college admission. For over 70 years the SAT I has included two sections, verbal and math, but the entire test will be overhauled and a new form of the exam will be introduced in the spring of 2005. The new test will include three sections, critical reading, math, and writing. Each section will be scored on a scale of 200–800 with a perfect score being 2400.

SAT II: The SAT IIs are subject-based tests that are required or recommended for admission at a variety of colleges and universities. If schools have a specific requirement or recommendation regarding SAT IIs, they will generally request three subject tests including writing, math, and one of the student's choosing. With the changes to the SAT I, which will be introduced in March 2005, the College Board may choose to eliminate the Writing test as it may be superfluous.

SCHOLARSHIPS: Correctly used, the term "scholarships" refers to grants awarded to students to recognize significant talent. Scholarships may be awarded on the basis of academic, athletic, artistic, or other personal talent. Grants awarded as part of a need-based financial aid package are not scholarships.

STUDY ABROAD: Once restricted to the financially well off or to those willing to sacrifice both time and money for the experience, study abroad opportunities have become prevalent on college campuses. Because financial aid is widely available to allow all students to participate in a study abroad program, and because colleges and universities have become much more willing to allow courses completed off campus and abroad to satisfy graduation requirements, virtually anyone can take part. Study abroad programs allow students to improve language skills and gain valuable cultural experience that enhances their ability to participate in today's global society and economy.

WAITING LIST: Something of a state of limbo in the world of college admissions, the waiting list status is the most uncertain and, in ways, the most frustrating. Certainly a decision that denies a student admission is the most disappointing but at least the student understands his status. For waiting list students, however, the admissions process continues and they remain uncertain as to their status with the institution. Students offered a position on the waiting list must indicate their desire to remain on the list. They then must wait until those students initially offered admission respond to their acceptance. If the school has any spaces left after those initially admitted respond, those on the waiting list will be considered again. Most schools will make waiting list decisions after May 1st but before the end of July. Students placed on a waiting list must secure a position at a school to which they have been offered admission, as the waiting list status is very uncertain and admission can never be taken for granted.

YIELD: A college's yield is the percentage of admitted students who enroll at their particular college or university. A school's yield can indicate its relative desirability. The nation's most competitive colleges and universities, for example, have very high yields, meaning most of those students who are admitted will choose to attend. A high yield, therefore, will generally prompt a school to have a lower acceptance rate.

Resources

ACT web site, 2003, *www.act.org.*

"Coaching Students with AD/HD," Flint Hill School Workshop, 2003.

College Board web site, 2003, *www.collegeboard.com.*

Columbia University web site, 2003, *www.columbia.edu.*

Educational Testing Service web site, 2003, *www.ets.org.*

Kenyon College web site, 2003, *www.kenyon.edu.*

Meeting College Costs, 2004 Edition, The College Board, 2003.

National Center for Education Statistics web site, 2003, *www.nces.ed.gov.*

National Association of Colleges and Empoyers web site, 2003. *www.naceweb.org.*

National Collegiate Athletic Association web site, 2003, *www.ncaa.org.*

National Merit Scholarship Corporation, Letter to Schools, 2003.

The New SAT and Your School, The College Board, 2003.

The Recentering of SAT Scales and Its Effects on Score Distributions and Score Interpretations, The College Board, 2002.

Virginia Tech web site, 2003, *www.ucc.vt.edu.*

Washington Research Council, 2003, *www.researchcouncil.org.*

State Council of Higher Education for Virginia web site, 2003, *www.schev.edu/students/salarycollege.asp.*

U.S. Department of Labor, Bureau of Labor Statistics web site, 2003, *www.bls.gov.*

Infoplease web site, 2003, *www.infoplease.com.*

LD OnLine web site, 2003, *www.ldonline.org.*

Index

CHOOSING A COLLEGE

For every question you have, Barron's guides have the right answers.

BARRON'S COLLEGE GUIDES

AMERICA'S #1 RESOURCE FOR EDUCATION PLANNING.

LOOKING FOR STUDY STRATEGIES THAT WORK? HAVE WE GOT SECRETS FOR YOU!

Student Success Secrets, 5th Edition

These sure-fire strategies can increase every student's test scores and raise their grades. Advice covers methods for forming good study habits, retaining information from reading, and taking useful classroom notes. There are also tips to help students do their best when taking exams.
$8.95, Canada $12.50, ISBN 0-7641-2007-7

B's & A's in 30 Days

Here's a sure-fire student success system for better grades, less stress, and greater self confidence. The book is divided into thirty short entertaining, instructive chapters— one for each day of the program. Students will learn how to set goals they can reach, study better in less time, take better classroom notes, and more. Amusing cartoon illustrations keep the mood appropriately light.
$11.95, Canada $16.95, ISBN 0-8120-9582-0

Barron's Educational Series, Inc.
250 Wireless Boulevard
Hauppauge, New York 11788

Visit our website at: barronseduc.com

(#9) R 3/04